THE CURSE OF CAIN

THE UNTOLD STORY OF JOHN WILKES BOOTH

THE CURSE OF CAIN

THE UNTOLD STORY OF JOHN WILKES BOOTH

by
Theodore J. Nottingham

APPALOOSA PRESS

Nicholasville, Kentucky

THE CURSE OF CAIN
By Theodore J. Nottimham

© 1997 by Theodore J. Nottingham

Book design: Apple Press, Inc.

ISBN 1-58006-021-8

Published by Appaloosa Press
106 North Main Street
Nicholasville, KY 40356-1234

Printed in the United States of America

Dedication

To my wife Rebecca whose presence in my life made possible the long journey during which this work was developed, and to our daughter Ashley whose talents reflect the best of her lineage.

Table of Contents

PREFACE

On the night of April 14, 1865, a gunshot from a small derringer interrupted the laughter at Ford's Theater and forever changed American history.

Hardly a week after the Confederacy's surrender at Appomatox, with Washington lavishly decorated to celebrate the end of the bloody Civil War, Abraham Lincoln slumped down in his chair never to regain consciousness.

The assassin leaped onto the stage crying out *"Sic Semper Tyrannis"* — "Thus always to tyrants." He was recognized immediately. Everyone in the theater knew him. Most had admired his charismatic presence on stage and hailed him as the finest actor of the era. A dozen members of the audience had chatted with him that very day.

At twenty-six years of age, John Wilkes Booth, son of the great tragedian Junius Brutus Booth and brother to Edwin, America's most acclaimed Hamlet, was the toast of Washington. His theatrical triumphs followed him from Richmond to Boston and his future was assured as a brilliant and beloved star.

In one terrible instant, it all vanished. Why did he throw his destiny away? Who was he behind the handsome face and winsome persona? What forces were at work at his side, opening the way for his entrance into the President's private box seat and cutting the telegraph wires between the capital and surrounding army posts? Did his story really end at the burning farmhouse? What happened to the lives of those who loved him?

Our history books have been silent over mysteries kept hidden for generations. Strange tales have come down to us through the friends and family of John Wilkes Booth that have yet to be told. Tales of secret societies, escape to foreign lands, children fathered after the father's presumed death…and the shadow of a curse, one recognized by Booth himself while on the run in the swamps near the Potomac.

Behold, Thou has driven me out this day from the face of the earth; and from Thy face shall I be hid; and I shall be a fugitive and a vagabond in the earth.

This ancient curse is strangely fitting to Booth's destiny as a result of his terrible deed. It may even have become a greater retribution than the accepted historical theory that his life was ended by a soldier's bullet.

But the impact of his terrible deed also reverberated down through the generations, overshadowing the lives of his descendants. I am one of them, his great-grandson thrice removed.

My great-grandmother was the granddaughter of the assassin of Abraham Lincoln. Her mother, Ogarita, was Booth's daughter. She was six years old when he pulled the trigger at Ford's Theater and became transformed from a revered matinee idol to a desperate fugitive and lonely wanderer upon the earth.

Booth's great-grandson, Charles Edward Clutts, my grandfather, is now in his nineties. For most of his life, he would not speak of our ancestor out of shame and concern for his own safety.

* * *

From earliest childhood, I had heard of the dark, brooding ancestor who left a bloody mark on American history. The tragic tale of John Wilkes Booth has intrigued me ever since. From my father's side of the family, I developed a great love for Abraham Lincoln with his homespun wisdom and compassion. Through the writings of Carl Sandburg and the poems of Walt Whitman, Lincoln became for me a shining light of the American spirit at its best.

On my mother's side, there was an altogether different influence. Carved in my grandfather's features were the dark, almond-shaped eyes and pitch black hair of the Booth family. His mother (my great-grandmother) was one of those powerful women of the theater who traveled across the country in the early part of this century presenting their art in the strangest places. She was theater incarnate, with the temper of Medusa and the glare of Zeus. In her later years, still full of fire, she ran a little theater in Keene, New Hampshire where she carried on the family tradition to the end of her life.

That family legacy was both grand and tragic. For she was the granddaughter of one of the most reviled personages of history. Her mother, Ogarita, was also an actress who openly wore a picture of her father in a locket around her neck until she died at the young age of thirty-two. That locket has been passed down to me and I recently dusted it off to show it to my daughter while initiating her into the drama of our ancestors.

Throughout my youth, I felt particularly drawn to the twenty-six year old matinee idol whose destiny was aborted by that horrific act. I too was drawn early on to the theater and thereby felt a sort of genetic connection with the Booths who in their day were the premiere American family of the theater. Also passed down through the generations was the brooding mood of the Booths whose Spanish ancestry and dramatic flair fused into intense character traits.

For years, I heard the tale of the murder, of the lone killer, of the epic manhunt, and of the final capture and death scene. In my teens, I studied the book written by my great-grandmother's sister, the journalist Izola Forrester. *This One Mad Act*, published in 1937, was based on forty years of relentless research into the saga of John Wilkes Booth. My great aunt interviewed the actual participants in those terrible events, old men haunted by memories that no history book has recorded. Inspired by her efforts and discoveries, I undertook a similar research, studying all the best historians on the subject. The result won a Lilly Historical Scholarship. More importantly, it convinced me that the stories our teachers taught us in school were not complete, and some were even falsified by those who had a stake in the retelling of American history.

It may be that no one will ever know the full truth on these matters. But there is a powerful story here that Americans ought to know about as part of their inheritance. Once the political issues and easy labels have been put aside, we are faced with a tragedy that would have made Shakespeare himself envious.

I have therefore taken the solid research that can be traced all the way back to the day of the assassination and, based on feasible conclusions, have added dramatic narrative to convey the emotional tone of the human experience behind the pictures of the history books. I believe that the story is best represented in this way for it is more dramatic than any play in which the Booths displayed their mighty talents. Most of all, this is a drama of human beings who found themselves caught up in a hurricane of colossal events that tore them from their cherished hopes and dreams.

They deserve to have their story remembered.

PART ONE

THE STORY

THE CURSE OF CAIN

PROLOGUE

1869 — The Arsenal Penitentiary Morgue

A dim ray of light from a flickering lantern seeped through the bottom of the door. Footsteps echoed in the darkness and heavy keys rattled, unlocking the heavy, narrow door. It opened with a loud screech and the light from the lantern spread into the room.

Four silhouettes huddled behind the bright light.

They slowly entered the narrow crypt. The figures held their coats tightly around them against the cold and dampness. An old man's voice whispered from the slowly advancing group.

"When did you exhume him?"

"This morning, as soon as we got your telegram."

The lantern revealed a wooden casket, muddy and rotting. The group gathered around it. Four faces peered from the shadows: A tormented elderly woman; an aristocratic young woman; an aging, dignified army Colonel, and a grim undertaker.

"Would you hold the lantern for me, Colonel?" the undertaker requested.

"Certainly."

The undertaker handed him the lantern and began to work at the side of the old coffin. The rusty nails slipped out easily from the aging, humid wood. As the side loosened, the old woman brought a trembling hand to her lips, prepared to hold back a gasp. The young lady became pale and nervous while the Colonel watched on tensely.

The oblong box loosened and a loud crack echoed through the vault. Slowly, the mortician lifted the top and slid it to the side.

"Well, here it is..."

Colonel Pedgram handed the lantern to the undertaker who shined it into the coffin. The old soldier twitched at the sight of the corpse. The women looked away with a sigh of horror. Remnants of brown flesh hung loosely from the grinning skull of the cadaver. Black hair had grown out of proportion and added a spectral look to the head which lay crooked over a broken neck.

"God Almighty! How are we to identify that thing?" the colonel muttered.

"Bein' dead three years will do that to you, sir," the undertaker stated with a touch of irony in his voice.

"Well, ladies?" the colonel asked his companions.

"That...looks like his black suit..." The young woman's voice trembled with disgust and uncertainty.

"What about you, Mrs. Booth? What do you say?"

"Colonel Pedgram...I cannot tell if that is my son!" she answered with tears in her eyes. "The hair seems to have a red tint to it, which he didn't have...I don't know!"

Visibly uncomfortable with this delicate situation, the colonel placed his hand on the old woman's shoulder to steady her.

"Let's see what the dental charts tell us," he stated as he pulled out an envelope from his coat pocket. The undertaker opened the corpse's jaws. Colonel Pedgram read the charts and leaned over the skeleton.

"Would you shine that light a bit more to the right, please. Thank you...Let me see here...One tooth filled on the upper...Yep, there it is all right. How about the leg? The leg ought to be broken. The left one."

The undertaker lifted the pantleg. The bone was clearly broken near the ankle.

"It's broken, no doubt about it."

Everyone examined it, uncomfortable in this eerie atmosphere and revolted by the unpleasant task.

"I guess this is all we can do. You think it's him, Miss Chapman?"

"Who else could it be?"

"What about you, Mrs. Booth?" the colonel asked the old woman. "Surely you understand the importance of this identification. We must be certain."

"Why? This won't bring back Mr. Lincoln."

"There are too many rumors circulating. Your assurance will eliminate all this nonsen...all this doubt. You'll be helping our country to heal sooner, Mrs. Booth."

Miss Chapman took her hand and tried to comfort her.

"Is it John?"

Mrs. Booth looked at the corpse. She brought a trembling handkerchief to her mouth. Colonel Pedgram exchanged glances with Miss Chapman, becoming impatient. The young lady opened her purse and pulled out a pair of small scissors. She cut a bit of hair from the skull, bravely resisting the repulsion of touching it. She wrapped the hair in a handkerchief and offered it to Mrs. Booth.

"I know how much he loved you," she whispered.

Mrs. Booth took the relic as tears ran down her cheeks.

"Is this your son, Mrs. Booth?" the Colonel asked in a raspy, demanding voice. She closed her eyes and clutched the bit of hair. The others awaited her answer patiently.

"I...I don't...Yes, it must be. It must be..."

Heartbroken, she wept bitterly. Colonel Pedgram motioned for the undertaker to close the coffin. He knew that the mystery would be buried unresolved.

ONE

The theater was packed on this warm spring evening. It wasn't that the play was so good or the actors well known. *Our American Cousin* was a light comedy typical of the fare presented by theatrical troupes across the country with just enough humorous lines to leave the audiences mildly content with the way they had spent their night out.

This night Ford's Theater was sold out because the President and his wife would be present in the state box right above the stage. Everybody who was anybody wanted to be with Abe Lincoln on his first relaxing evening since the horror of the Civil War had finally ended. Like the cherry blossoms around the city opening to the April sunshine, it was time for new life to rise out of the darkness of the past four years.

The audience was in their Sunday best, eagerly awaiting the entrance of the true star of the show. A low hum of whispering voices filled the theater. John Ford, the owner and manager, watched from the wings, eyes sparkling with pleasure. There hadn't been this much excitement in his establishment since the great Junius Brutus Booth and his charismatic sons graced the stage with a stunning presentation of Shakespeare's *Julius Caesar*. Now that the war was over, Ford knew that ticket sales would once again make it possible for him to produce the classics he loved so much.

He stepped back from the curtain and turned his attention to the activities backstage. The cast was busily putting the last touches on make-up and costumes and the crew hurried back and forth with set pieces. The excitement was a thrill to behold for the aging manager. This was his joy and he could hardly wait to witness his actors entertain an audience starved for escape and laughter.

Ford moved through the hustle and bustle, soaking in the nervous energy of his employees. He noticed a silhouette near the performer's exit door. A man stood there as still as a statue, creating a strange contrast to the activity around him. Ford peered through the dim light, trying to make out who it was that seemed so detached from the pre-curtain madness.

"John!" he called out, recognizing the gallant features of his favorite actor.

The man turned to him, startled.

"Are you here to see the performance? I tell you, it's never been better."

The man nodded without a word. Ford came up to him and patted him on the shoulder.

"We're back in business, John. Are you ready to give us Hamlet again?"

Dark, intense eyes—large and almond shaped with pupils black as olives—fell upon the manager. Ford stepped back involuntarily. He had never seen such a harsh glare pouring out of the handsome features of his friend, John Wilkes Booth.

"The War's over, John. It's time to enjoy life again," Ford said with a smile, hoping to cheer him up. In all his years around dramatic individuals, he knew of no one who could match young Booth's brooding intensity. Though hard to take in a social situation, it sure generated a powerful presence on the stage and great income for the theater. It hadn't been that way before the war. Young Booth was gregarious and full of life, often the life of the party. Not anymore.

"I don't have a single seat left. You'll have to watch from the wings."

Booth looked away toward the darkened stage. Ford wondered if his star performer had been drinking again. His father, genius that he was, had long ago become a slave to the bottle. The poison was so rampant among his actors that Ford knew all the signs: the irascible personality, the fits of rage, the loss of concentration, and finally the breakdown of the actor's most important tool—his memory.

John Booth was one performer whom Ford couldn't let sink into that hopeless abyss. He was too talented, too attractive to the ladies in the audience, and his future was immeasurable. He was the great actor of his generation at only twenty-six years of age.

"Take care of yourself, John," the manager whispered with paternal concern. Booth glanced back at him in surprise and then moved off into the shadows. Ford could never have imagined that this was the last time he would ever see him.

Dressed in black from head to foot, Booth vanished in the darkness. He walked briskly through the underbelly of the theater, heading for the lobby. Heads turned as he passed by the dressing rooms and carpenter's shop. From his Spanish ancestry, he had received curly, raven black hair and sharply chiseled features. An elegant mustache further emphasized his magnetic and dramatic expression. The man was the incarnation of the classic actor, the heir to the throne of the premiere family of the American theater. Even his brother Edwin, already acclaimed in Europe as a phenomenal talent, couldn't match his explosive stage presence.

Fellow performers were often frightened and sometimes hurt when facing him in staged sword fights. Booth was an agile athlete with the instincts of a tiger. He approached his dueling scenes with virtually uncontrolled ferocity.

Now this same fiery energy coursed through his entire body as he moved swiftly to the front of the building. Members of the crew who happened by instinctively stepped out of his way, yielding to his determined march toward his dark destiny.

The President's carriage pulled up in front of the theater. True to his humble origins, Lincoln insisted on the minimum of formalities, and a foreigner who wouldn't recognize his lanky figure could hardly have guessed at his high position. A man and his wife were simply out on the town with friends. Their companion, Major Rathbone, was the closest thing to a bodyguard. No soldiers accompanied them, no fanfare, no protection.

John Ford greeted the great man and his plump little wife at the door and guided them to the staircase leading to the Presidential boxseat. People milling about the lobby smiled and nodded respectfully. Lincoln's lack of airs made everyone comfortable. In that moment, even he forgot that he was perhaps the most hated man in the country. Too much blood had been spilled and too much destroyed for forgiveness and sane reasoning to take place. It would be generations before Abraham Lincoln was universally recognized as perhaps the country's finest president.

The lobby was empty by the time Booth approached the staircase. The play was in progress and waves of light laughter drifted in from behind the closed doors. The actor was alone with his thoughts and his devotion to a lost cause. He stepped out into the night air.

The stars sparkled above, speaking to him directly from eternity. However, their message of peace and goodwill went unheard. He knew exactly when he was going to strike. Early in the second act, there would be only one actor on stage. His line would cause loud laughter and in the midst of the reaction few would hear the sound of a gunshot.

Booth had never killed a man before. In the role of Brutus, he had drawn a knife on his beloved and tyrannical emperor, but the bard's lyrical poetry made him feel fully justified. A shutter of nervous energy caused him to twitch. He took a deep breath and forced himself to relax in the same way he had done so many times before opening night. It didn't work. The knot in his stomach would not go away. A desire to burn the discomfort out with strong drink swept over him.

He hesitated, then hurried across the street toward a small saloon. The bar was dark with only a few patrons scattered throughout the room. The bartender recognized the new arrival and immediately poured a shotglass of his finest whiskey.

"Thank you kindly, Jim," the actor whispered in his famous baritone voice. He swallowed the poison without a blink and slid the empty glass back to the bartender.

"Everything all right?" Jim asked with some concern. He had seen the actor drink heavily before and he felt a twinge of guilt at participating in the destruction of such a striking and talented gentleman.

Booth threw back a whiskey. The liquid burned his throat and chest in a familiar, relieving sensation that had long been part of his life, even at this early age. The poison carried with it the magic of forgetfulness—forgetting the early failures and humiliations of his acting career; forgetting the insanity of his father, the great

Junius Brutus Booth, the most highly acclaimed actor as well as one of the most drunken lunatics of his generation; forgetting his jealousy of his brother Edwin whose melancholic temperament made the ideal Hamlet; even the forgetfulness of his newfound fame that made him the talk of the town from Washington to Richmond.

He had taken to the stage at the age of seventeen and soon was a sensation in theaters everywhere. When he opened as Richard the Third at Grover's Theatre on April 11, 1863, he was billed as: "The Pride of the American people—The youngest tragedian in the world—a star of the first magnitude—son of the great Junius Brutus Booth—brother and artistic rival of Edwin Booth."

The newspapers of the day hailed him as a "complete triumph." A critic wrote: "His youth, originality, and superior genius have not only made him popular but established him in the hearts of Washington people as a great favorite." Fellow actors said that he possessed "extraordinary presence and magnetism."

He was universally considered the most handsome man to grace the stage. "He was the idol of women" said British actor Charles Wyndham. Lady Anne Hartley Gilbert observed that he was "a very handsome man, perhaps the handsomest I ever saw."

The *Washington Chronicle* announced that "this handsome, passionate boy as an actor has more of the native fire and fury of his great father than any of his family...He has more of the old man's power in one performance than Edwin can show in a year." The *Boston Daily Advertiser* called him "the actor in the country" and the *Baltimore Sun* proclaimed: "an actor with the suddenness of a meteor now illuminates the dramatic horizon."

He was also beloved by his fellow actors. Backstage, he was respected as "the gentlest man" in the business. In rehearsal, he was always considerate of the other actors, and if he had a suggestion to make, he always made it with the utmost courtesy.

They called him the handsomest man in America, and with his energetic athletic skills and natural abilities, he could steal a scene from the best of them. But he didn't have to, because he was already John Booth, the matinee idol of the era. Women swooned at his presence, and men envied his Greek god frame. He had it all and yet he needed to throw back that whiskey and feel it burn a hole in his soul through which all his painful feelings could temporarily vanish.

John was on the side that had lost the war. Born and bred in Baltimore, he loved the genteel southern culture where he had first found fame on the stage. He hated the North, especially the lanky president from Illinois. Lincoln was a dictator of the worst kind as far as he was concerned, a usurper who had torn up the Constitution of the United States. The right of each state to choose its own ways, free from a distant government's control, was as close as he came to religious devotion.

The horror and atrocities of the last four years had crippled his soul forever. He could hardly bring himself to put on his greasepaint and strut upon the stage while men were dying by the thousands and a whole culture was falling to its knees, never to rise again. The slavery issue was not a concern to him. He hadn't thought it through and like many others remained content with the way things were. Among his closest friends, he numbered young Henry, the son of his black nanny, Sarah, who was dearly beloved by the whole family. Yet he had failed to catch the vision of equality and freedom for all God's children.

A third whiskey insured that his mind was numbed of these disturbing thoughts and his courage focused on the decisive act he was about to carry out. John Booth had fought realistically on the stage and scared some of his fellow actors with his aggressive swordplay, but the blood was fake and the dead man always got up when the curtain came down. This time there would be no getting up again.

He shifted the position of the little derringer in his belt. The small weapon carried one lead bullet in its chamber — all that was needed to change history and avenge his beloved and desecrated South. This one bullet would insure his role in history as the hero of a just cause, or so he thought.

He checked his watch. The play was beginning. He knew his cue was not until the second act. He leaned against the bar, smoldering in nervous tension and strange feelings of sorrow and despair. This was not what he had planned to do. He had tried to kidnap Lincoln several weeks before with the aim of exchanging him for Confederate prisoners. The attempt had been a failure and something more drastic was now required.

He caught sight of his reflection in the mirror behind the bar. The grim look in his eyes stirred a memory of his childhood. A day long ago when a similar disturbance had ruffled his soul.

He was still a youth living in a happy world of fantasy on his father's farm. One day, a Gypsy fortune teller came through town. John's sister Asia persuaded him to have her read his palm. The mysterious old woman's words were engraved in his memory.

"Ah, you've a bad hand, the lines all criss-cross. It's full enough of sorrow—full of trouble—trouble in plenty, everywhere I look. You'll break hearts, they'll mean nothing to you. You'll die young and leave many to mourn you, many to love you too, but you'll be rich, generous, and free with your money. You're born under an unlucky star. You've got in your hand a thundering crowd of enemies—not one friend—you'll make a bad end, and have plenty to love you afterwards. You'll have a fast life—short, but a grand one.

"I've never seen such a worse hand, and I wish I hadn't seen it, but every word I've told is true by the signs. You'd best turn a missionary or priest and try to escape it."

A man came up to the melancholic actor lost in thought at the bar.

"Are you playing this evening, Mister Booth?"

"Does it look like it?" Booth responded as he called for another shot of poison.

"Just a question, Mister Booth. I'm one of your admirers."

"Are you?" Booth said grimly without looking at him.

"Yes sir. I saw you as Richard the Third. The best performance since your father played it in Boston."

"You thought I was as good as my father?" Booth turned to him with sudden interest.

"Your father was the greatest of his time. But you bring to it your own genius. I've seen you in "The Marble Heart" as well. Your talent blossoms with every new role, it seems."

"I take it you're not a drama critic."

"No sir, I'm not. Just an ordinary theater goer. My business takes me to different cities and I've seen a lot of actors. Your brother, for instance. I've seen his Hamlet several times."

"My brother *is* Hamlet," Booth said with a sarcasm mixed with sorrow. He knew that his brother would never forgive him for what he was about to do. He'd voted for Lincoln twice.

"You'll be the pride of the Booth family. No doubt some day

your King Lear will outshine them all."

Booth looked at him intensely. His large dark eyes covered over with a distant mist.

"I won't have to wait forty years to play that part. There's a bit of King Lear in me already."

The man was taken aback by the tragedy radiating from his soul. He smiled awkwardly, bid him farewell, and hurried away, unable to sustain the weight of the man's darkness.

Booth checked his watch again. The time was approaching. Another memory arose in his mind, not of adulation and applauding crowds as he was used to, but of secret meetings and somber faces. That other part of his life that was even more important to him than the theater. He recalled the last time he had met with his mysterious brothers, all of whom as devoted as he was to the cause.

"If you go to the east, I will go to the west. Let there be no strife between mine and thine, for we be brethren." So went the ritual of this most secret of secret societies. Booth and his friend John Surratt had smuggled documents for the organization across the Mason-Dixon line, and even into Canada. The Knights of the Golden Circle were funded by great wealth and power. Their mission transcended the basic issues of the War. Key members were leaders in the international Freemasonry societies and had ties with high officials of foreign governments, especially in England.

Booth's dramatic inclinations, idealistic convictions and attractions to things occult had made him a perfect initiate. Now his commitments to the brotherhood were being tested to the extreme.

He looked at his watch again. The time had come.

Just at that moment, a soldier entered the bar, sneaking in

with the telltale look of an addict in need of his fix. He caught sight of the handsome actor and immediately looked away, attempting to hide a terrified reaction. The man's face was a map of self-destruction, haggard and skeletal-like. He sat at the bar and ordered a drink in a tone of desperation.

Booth adjusted his black hat, tightened his leather gloves around his fingers, and headed off for an entrance that would resonate through history.

TWO

Two silhouettes stood in the shadows of a wealthy residential district on the outskirts of the city. Lewis Paine, a tall, muscular former soldier stared at a mansion across the street. Crouching behind him was a nervous and unkempt little man, David Herold.

Herold pulled out a watch.

"Now?" Paine asked in an excited whisper.

"No, not yet," Herold stuttered in terror. "I wonder what Mister Booth is doing right now."

"Watching a play," Paine answered with a sinister smirk.

"Do you think he'll have any trouble?"

"Will you quit shiverin' like an old maid, damn it! Of course he won't have any trouble. It's all set up. Lincoln's sittin' there ready to be picked off. Same as our great Secretary of State across the street."

They waited impatiently. The silence of the neighborhood was grating on their frayed nerves.

"Is it time?"

Herold looked at his watch.

"Another minute. Aren't you nervous, Paine?"

"Hell, no. I been killin' Yankees for years. This is just one more."

He looked down at his terrified companion.

"I can't figure out how you got involved with all this, Herold. What we needed was some real soldiers."

"This ain't no battlefield out here," Herold said resentfully. "It took brains, maneuvrin', knowin' important people."

"That don't explain why you ever crawled out of your rat hole."

Herold smacked him in the arm. Paine grabbed him by the collar and lifted him off the ground. He caught himself just before ramming Herold into the tree.

"I ain't got time to mess with the likes of you. I got a job to do."

Paine dropped him and turned his attention toward the house.

"I'll deal with you later!" he muttered.

Herold glared at him. His whole body quivered with hatred and terror.

"Is it time?" Paine asked again.

"Yes! Yes!" Herold cried out, looking at his watch.

Paine cracked his knuckles, smiled arrogantly at Herold, and walked off toward the house. Herold watched him as he shivered uncontrollably.

Suddenly, he hurried off toward two horses tied to a nearby fence. He mounted his horse, looked back for a last glance at Paine with only the slightest shadow of guilt, and galloped off into the darkness.

Paine knocked at the door of a large mansion. An old nurse peered through the opening.

"Is Mister Seward in?"

"He is ill, sir. He's had an accident and is bed-ridden."

"I must see him. Doctor Verdi sent me."

Paine stepped into the house, forcing his way past the woman. She followed him, trying to stop him as he headed toward the staircase.

"He cannot see you, sir! You are not to come in here!"

Hearing the noise of Paine's heavy boots on the wooden stairway, a young man came out of the room in which lay the Secretary of State and hurried to the top of the stairs.

"I'm sorry, sir. You cannot..." the youth ordered.

"I've been directed by Doctor Verdi to leave a package."

"I'll be glad to take it for him."

"I must give it to him personally."

"If you can't leave it with me, you'll just have to be on your way."

"Well, if I can't see him..." Paine said as he started back down the stairs.

Suddenly, he turned around, drawing a revolver. He pulled the trigger but it misfired. Enraged, he charged the young man and smashed the pistol-butt into his head. As the youth sank to his knees, Paine struck him repeatedly, terrific blows that broke the pistol. He hurled the useless weapon at the nurse and drew a huge bowie knife.

The nurse shrieked frantically.

Paine raced into the room where the Secretary of State lay in bed, wearing a surgical collar around his neck for a broken jaw.

Seward's right arm was in a cast as well. He turned to the attacker, terrified, unable to move.

The first swing of the knife slashed the old man's cheek. Seward gasped and rolled across the bed to evade the blows. The bedsprings creaked as Paine leapt on the helpless man and grabbed him by the hair to expose his throat. In the heat of animal rage, Paine slashed at the neck-brace.

Seward tossed wildly as Paine stuck the knife in his shoulder. The old man managed to roll off the mattress, tumbling onto the floor in a heap of bedcloth and blood.

Two men raced into the room and took hold of Paine as the nurse continued her hysterical screaming. Paine turned on the newcomers, kicking and slashing. He gashed one of them with the blood-stained knife and crashed over the furniture with the other assailant.

Paine beat the man unconscious and dashed out of the room, leaving behind a ransacked room splattered in blood.

* * *

Thunderous laughter and applause echoed from the stage, spilling into the alley that led to the side entrance of Ford's Theater. A cat hurried across the dimly lit path dotted with mud puddles.

A silhouette appeared in the misty darkness. The dark, handsome features of John Wilkes Booth became visible in the shadowed light. He came to the side entrance and opened the door. The sound of the happy audience burst out into the alley and faded away as the door closed behind him.

He walked through the dim backstage light. Several stagehands smiled at him as he headed for the lobby and up the staircase.

Booth was calm, though a powerful determination burned in his eyes. At the top of the stairs, he opened another door. He entered the back of the theater's balcony. The packed house was laughing at the performance on stage, a strange contrast to the deadly harshness in Booth's features.

He stopped and watched the play. He looked over at the little white door leading to the State Box. The chair next to the door where the guard was expected to be sitting was empty.

Pearls of sweat glistened on his forehead as Booth slowly moved toward the President's box. Booth stopped again and watched the play. He scanned the audience for soldiers. None were present.

Booth entered the short passageway between the two doors leading to the President's box. He breathed deeply as his heart pounded in a matter that no opening night had ever caused. He pulled out his small derringer.

Through a hole in the door, Booth watched Lincoln's hand gently pressing his wife's hand. Suddenly, there was a profound silence in the theater.

Only one actor stood on stage.

"Well, I guess I know enough to turn you inside out, old gal— you sockdologizing old man trap!"

A muffled gunshot exploded through the laughter. A vague hush fell over the audience. A shrill scream burst through the silence. Was it still part of the play? The confused actor on stage tried to stay in character.

In the President's box, Booth struggled with Major Rathbone. He slashed him with a knife and leapt onto the railing that was decorated with the union flag. As he jumped onto the stage, his spur caught in the folds of the flag. He landed awkwardly.

With a strange calm, Booth limped along the edge of the footlights, facing the audience.

He shouted with an actor's power of projection:

"*Sic Semper Tyrannis!*"

He crossed the stage, walking neither slowly nor particularly rapidly, and vanished backstage. Another moment of incredulous silence filled the theater.

"He has killed the President!" a woman screamed.

Another instant of stunned silence hovered over the audience. Then a deluge of horror, cries, shouts, terror and confusion broke loose. People jumped up and ran throwing chairs aside, women fainted, others were trampled. A crowd of men rushed onto the stage.

Booth shoved his way past stagehands and actors. One of the theater's carpenters, a long acquaintance of Booth and a Southern sympathizer, swung open the side door and cleared people out of the area.

In the alley, a young boy awaited, holding the reins of a saddled horse. Booth burst out of the theater, pushed the boy aside, and jumped on the horse. An officer chasing him appeared in the alley and grabbed the reins. The two men struggled.

Booth managed to kick him out of the way and galloped off into the night. He raced through the dark streets of the capital like a fury from hell. The grimace of pain on his face and a distorted leg hanging out of the stirrup made his appearance all the more unnatural and demonic. The city's peace belied the hurricane of horror and anger soon to be unleashed across the nation.

Booth slowed his horse as he came around a corner, slipping on the cobblestone. A figure suddenly appeared ahead of him, walking in his direction. The silhouette moved into the light of a street lamp. He was a man in his late twenties, Bill Andrews, a childhood friend.

Booth jerked his horse to a halt.

"Billy!"

Bill Andrews hurried toward him.

"John!"

"It's done, Billy...The South is avenged!" Booth said through teeth gritted in agony.

Bill Andrews looked out into the darkness, petrified.

"Are you all right?"

"No, damn it all! I think I broke my leg."

"Let me see."

"The left one."

Bill Andrews hurried around the horse and gently touched Booth's leg.

"I caught it in the flag..."

He let out a muffled yell as his friend touched the broken bone.

"You can't travel with this leg, John!"

Distant sounds of angry voices rose in the darkness. Booth started to move on. Bill grabbed the reins.

"Wait, Johnny, wait!" he cried out frantically.

He took off his scarf and wrapped it around Booth's ankle.

"Hurry!" Booth muttered, closing his eyes in pain.

"I've got nothing to hold it with!" Andrews said frantically.

"Be careful! It's killing me."

Andrews tore a pin from his vest and fastened it to the scarf. He reached up and took hold of Booth's hand.

"God be with you, John!"

"Remember our friendship, Billy."

They looked at each other one last time.

The echo of shouts came nearer. Booth spurred his horse onward. Bill Andrews watched him gallop away, tears rolling down his cheeks.

Cavalry soldiers were forcing their mounts through the panicked crowds gathered outside the theater. Soldiers brutally pushed actors and audience members out of the building. Other soldiers were fighting their way into the theater. Absolute panic had taken the place of the merriment that had been present a few moments before.

Across the street from the theater, in the living room of the Peterson house, anguished men paced quietly in the packed room. They kept turning to a partially opened door in the back of the room. The frantic yelling of the crowds shook the windows.

The Secretary of War, Edwin Stanton, appeared in the doorway of the back room and gazed grimly at the waiting men. With his long beard and heavy features, he was the very image of rigid domination. In that moment, he was the most powerful man in the country.

"How much longer does he have, Mr. Secretary?"

"A few hours maybe...Where's the Vice President, damn it!"

"What's the news on the murderer, sir?"

"I've ordered all roads out of Washington blockaded."

"Do you know who it is?" another man asked.

"No," Stanton curtly responded.

"I thought he'd been recognized."

"Not positively. We're in the process of investigating that. He's a reb, that's certain."

"Isn't he an actor at Ford's?"

"I told you we don't know yet! When it's definite, I'll have it dispatched to all points."

He walked back into the other room with the gait of an angry bear.

* * *

Booth rode madly through the countryside. He came to a bridge across which an iron gate had been lowered. Two union soldiers stood guard.

Booth slowed his horse and trotted up to the bridge. The soldiers approached him.

"Who are you?"

"My name is Paul Stewart," Booth replied with the confidence of a skilled actor.

"Where are you from?"

"The city."

"Where are you going?"

"I'm going home. I live in Charles County."

"Don't you know it's against orders for anyone to pass barriers after nine?"

"I had to work late this evening."

The sergeant studied him for a moment, spit out a wad of tobacco, and nodded for the soldier to raise the gate.

Booth patiently watched the gate rise, skillfully hiding the agony and tension boiling in his body. He slowly moved his horse forward. As he passed by, the soldier noticed his left leg hanging out of the stirrup. He looked at it curiously but made nothing of it.

The gate lowered as Booth trotted away. Once in the shadows, he shuddered as he touched his leg. He then kicked his horse into a gallop.

In the distance, a boy walked alongside the road. Booth slowed his mount as he approached. The dark figure reined in next to him.

"Have you seen another rider pass by?"

"No, sir. I haven't seen anybody."

Booth looked back into the shadows behind him, worried. He jerked the reins and tore off at a gallop.

Another rider approached the bridge. The soldiers stood up, surprised to be disturbed twice in one night on this little traveled path.

"Your name?" the sergeant asked.

"Smith, sir," David Herold answered, mud-splattered and terrified.

The soldiers checked his papers and waved him on through.

The boy walking along the road looked up to see Herold galloping toward him. He was distressed to see the rider pull up to his side.

"Has a rider been by here?"

"Yes, sir. He went that'a'way."

Herold raced off into the darkness. The boy watched him disappear. He then took off into the woods to avoid any more passers-by.

Booth was galloping at full speed when he heard the sound of another rider behind him. He slowed to a trot and moved to the side of the road. The silhouette galloped toward him.

As he passed by him, Booth moved out of the shadows.

"Herold!" Booth called out.

Herold swung his horse around.

"Oh, sweet Jesus! I thought I'd never find you!"

Booth came up alongside him.

"Where's Paine?"

"I don't know," Herold said with hesitation. "We got separated and he must have lost his way."

Booth whipped his horse into a trot. Herold frantically tried to keep up with him. Once at his side, Herold looked at him anxiously, waiting for the news.

"Pray for the man's soul, Herold."

Herold sat up in his saddle and let out a rebel yell.

"When the dead is at rest, let his remembrance rest," Booth mumbled, "and be comforted for him, when his spirit is departed from him."

"What?"

"The book of Ecclesiastes."

Herold looked at him curiously. He noticed the pain etched on his features.

"What's the matter?"

"We must change our plans. I broke my damn leg. I can't walk from the farm to the boat."

"How did you do that, Mister Booth?" Herold cried out in a panic.

"My spur caught in the flag when I jumped. Thank God Ned was there to clear the way."

"What are you going to do now?"

"Get the hell down to Surrattsville!"

They galloped on, pushing their mounts at full speed.

* * *

Major Eckert, a bear of a man with a temper to match his size, hurried into the Peterson living room where everyone was sadly awaiting the President's passing. He made his way through the mourning men, looking anxiously for someone.

He approached the door leading to the bedroom. One of the men standing nearby stopped him.

"What do you think you're doing?" he asked in an angry whisper.

"I gotta see Secretary Stanton. It's urgent."

"You'll have to wait until he comes out."

Eckert took hold of the door knob.

"The President is dying in there! Show some respect, soldier!"

The officer turned on the man whom he towered over and threatened him with an angry glare. The door suddenly opened and a doctor looked out.

"Will you gentlemen please keep your voices down!"

"Doc, I gotta get to Stanton," the major said, disregarding his request for quiet.

"Are you referring to the Secretary of War?"

"'Course I am! Tell him it's Major Eckert."

Stanton noticed him and came out of the room.

"It's all right, doctor," he said coldly.

He stepped into the living room. As he closed the door, the officer caught a glimpse of a lanky corpse lying on the bed. The pillow was red with blood.

Stanton and Major Eckert moved off into a corner.

"What is it, Major?"

"All the telegraph wires leading out of the city have been cut!"

"What the hell are you talking about?"

"Two lines in the main battery have been crossed and shorted everything."

Stanton stroked his large beard, reflecting on the news.

"The secret wire to Old Point is still in operation," the Major whispered.

Stanton thought for a moment, glancing at the others in the room.

"Contact Old Point and have them telegraph back to all outly-
ing forts. Tell them to get Colonel Baker out here immediately."

"What about that actor?" Eckert whispered. "A lot of witnesses
are convinced it's him. Should we send his name out with the dispatches?"

"No. I want positive identification first."

"But there seems to be no..."

Stanton glared at him. Eckert interrupted himself and silently
read the look in Stanton's eyes.

In the dark barroom, at table in the furthest corner, a drunken
soldier was pouring himself yet another shot of whiskey. John
Parker was a frail, sickly man dressed in a private's uniform. His
face was prematurely aged by alcohol. Torment was etched on his
features.

An old man came to his table and sat next to him. He
observed his miserable condition.

"I heard it said that ol' Abe himself knew this was gonna happen sooner or later."

John Parker stared into his glass. He took a drink.

"It could have been stopped."

"Nah...It had to happen. Fate decides these things. Us poor
devils here below, we just gotta bear it all. And in seventy-five
years, I still ain't seen any purpose to it."

Parker suddenly threw his head into his arms and wept violently. The old man looked at him, bewildered. He put his hand on
Parker's shoulder.

"Hey, come on now. There's nothin' anybody could have done
to stop it."

Parker turned to him, his face ravaged by tears.

"Yes, there is! There is! I was assigned to guard the entrance
to the State Box!"

"You! Tonight?" the old man cried out, horror-stricken.

"I can't understand it! The Secretary of War personally sent me the orders...I was already on probation for drinking on duty. I...I can't help myself!"

He wept uncontrollably. Aghast, the old man rose and hurried away.

THREE

David Herold ran out of the Surrattsville tavern carrying a large bag. A ragged and exhausted Booth waited nearby on his horse, holding the reins of Herold's mount.

"Do you have everything?"

Herold jumped on his horse and opened the bag.

"Field glasses, carbine, and two bottles of brandy. Mrs. Surratt's always been a thoughtful one."

"We'll have to get to a doctor, Herold. The pain is too much."

Herold looked at him, terrified.

"How can we, Mister Booth? Union soldiers is gonna be all over these parts. We gotta get down to Bryantown!"

"We have no choice. If I don't get this leg taken care of, I won't make it to the boat."

Booth feverishly opened a bottle of brandy.

"I bought a horse awhile back from a doctor who lives about four hours from here. He's a good man. He'll help us."

He took a swig of brandy and grimaced as the alcohol burned his parched throat. He handed the bottle to Herold who put it back in the bag.

Booth looked up at the sparkling stars, sponging the sweat and mud from his brow.

"O! that this too too solid flesh would melt, thaw and resolve itself into a dew; Or that the Everlasting had not fixed His canon against self-slaughter!" he whispered hoarsely. "O God! O God! How weary, stale, flat, and unprofitable seem to me all the uses of this world."

Herold was made all the more nervous by his behavior. Booth continued to stare at the heavens, transfixed with melancholy.

"Shall we move on, Mister Booth?"

Booth took a deep breath, and with a resolute shout whipped his horse into a gallop.

* * *

A silhouette sat near a window, head sagging toward his chest. A little note card lay on a table near the fireplace. The scribbling read: *April 14th - 2 PM. Do not wish to disturb you. Would like an interview. J.W.B.*

Several empty bottles on the floor surrounded the drunken man. A frantic knock at the door interrupted the silence.

"Mister Vice-President! Are you there?"

The massive head of Vice-President Andrew Johnson raised itself and turned toward the door, red eyes filled with gloom.

"Mister Vice-President!!"

A fist pounded violently on the door. The vice-president would not answer.

In the office of the war department, officials conversed in nervous, hushed tones in the dim light. Confusion was everywhere. Major Eckert burst into the room, followed by another officer.

"How long have the lines been restored?"

"About three minutes, sir," the officer answered.

Eckert hurried to the telegraph operator.

"Two hours! Damn it! He could be halfway through Virginia by now!"

Officials gathered around the telegraph operator.

"Mister Stanton wants this message dispatched: President's murderer is John Wilkes Booth. Description: about five feet nine, black hair, eyes brown. Mustache of moderate size. Wearing a black coat, dark pants.

"Send this out to Winchester, Harper's Ferry, Cumberland, Baltimore, Annapolis, Acquia Creek, and Relay House."

"What about Port Tobacco Road, down in the flat foot of Maryland?" an officer inquired.

"He wouldn't go that way, not if he didn't want to get caught."

"But Port Tobacco Road is between the Potomac and the Patuxant..."

"We got no time for debates, Lieutenant! There are five hundred detectives in and around Washington looking for the son of a bitch. Colonel Baker will be here shortly to get the Secret Service moving. Mister Stanton wants every damn regiment in the city sent out through southern Maryland. Gentlemen, this is the largest manhunt in history, and we're going to catch him before his murder weapon has had time to cool off!"

* * *

Dr. Mudd's home was in an isolated countryside, illuminated by pale moonlight. The silence was broken only by the monotonous sound of crickets.

A match burst into flame, revealing Herold's terrified features as he lit a lantern. He held it up to Booth who shivered with pain in his saddle.

Booth took out a mirror and false whiskers from his saddlebag. He rapidly pasted on his disguise. Herold watched in amazement as the actor changed his features.

"Have you ever been to the theater, Herold?"

"Sure. I'd go whenever I had some money left over at the end of the week. I seen you three or four times, Mister Booth. I couldn't understand a whole lot of that old fashioned talk, but I really liked them sword fights. I thought you was actually gonna kill that other prince in that one play...What was it? With the ghost and that skull you picked up."

"You saw my Hamlet?"

"Why sure. Them historic plays was my favorites. I'm kind of a student of history you might say."

"Well, David Herold, you are now a part of history. You'll be remembered along with the heroes of Thermopylae and Troy. You'll stand before the wonder and admiration of the world as a noble lover of liberty and justice. You'll stand alongside our fathers who rebelled against the oppression of the mother country."

Herold smiled uneasily. Booth put on the finishing touches to his make-up.

"For now, we must put on a fine performance for the good doctor. Remember what I told the players at the court of Denmark: "Suit the action to the word, the word to the action; with this special observance, that you o'erstep not the modesty of nature."

Herold led the horses out of the woods toward a roadside gate. A large farmhouse rose a few yards away. The gate creaked open and Herold led the horses up the long drive. Several dogs barked in the darkness.

Booth remained calm, though his face was rigid with tension as he fought the pain. Herold approached the door and knocked. A light appeared in the house as someone came downstairs.

"Who's there?" a voice called out.

"My companion has fallen from his horse and hurt his leg.

He's in a lot of pain. Could you please help us?"

Dr. Samuel Mudd opened the door and looked at the two strangers suspiciously. He noticed Booth's leg hanging crooked out of the stirrup.

"Help me bring him into the house, I'll have a look at him."

They carried Booth to a sofa and laid him down carefully. Dr. Mudd removed the boot as Booth cringed in agony. He examined the leg.

"The fibula is broken and the flesh badly lacerated. I'll have to set that leg before you can walk again."

"How long will it take?" Booth asked through clenched teeth.

"You'll have to stay off your feet for at least two days. You're welcome to stay with us for awhile."

"All right, doctor. Fix the damn thing."

Dr. Mudd left the room to gather his instruments. Herold could hardly control his panic.

"Soldiers are gonna be crawling all over these parts in no time! We've got to get across the Potomac soon!"

"I've ridden nearly sixty miles with the bone of my leg tearing the flesh at every jump!" Booth replied, making it clear that he was going to take a rest. "You'll give us away if you don't calm yourself."

He lowered his voice to a barely audible whisper.

"Our friends have put out decoys to guide the soldiers away from us. We have time."

The sound of footsteps drew their attention. Booth looked up to find a silhouette staring back at him. An English gentleman, spending the night as the doctor's guest, stared at him with a strange, impassive look. A knowing glance passed between the two men that said everything and nothing. It was so subtle that Herold missed the mysterious familiarity.

Dr. Mudd re-appeared. He sensed the tension in the room, but didn't know what to make of it.

"This gentleman is a guest here. Mister William Bartlett, may I present Mister..."

"Stewart. Paul Stewart."

"And aaah..." Dr. Mudd continued, turning to Herold.

"Smith. Pleasure to meet you, sir," Herold said awkwardly.

"Good evening, gentlemen," Bartlett stated with a heavy upper class English accent. "Pity to make your acquaintance under such importune circumstances. May I be of assistance, Doctor?"

"That would be kind of you," the doctor responded as he studied Booth's leg.

"I can fashion splints rather well," the Englishman offered.

"Oh? That would be..."

"This bandbox will do," the guest observed with expert eyes.

Bartlett set to work. Booth watched him intensely, then turned his attention to Dr. Mudd's operation.

Mrs. Mudd appeared at the top of the stairs. She observed the scene, a strange intuition filling her with anxiety. Then she hurried away to retrieve a bottle of brandy.

The three men carried Booth up the stairs into a bedroom as he shivered with agony. They laid him on the bed. Herold placed the brandy bottle provided by Mrs. Mudd on a desk beside the bed.

"He must rest now," the doctor ordered.

Booth took Dr. Mudd 's hand and looked into his face, eyes glazed with pain.

"Thank you, Doctor...You're..."

Dr. Mudd patted his hand, checked his feverish forehead, and left the room. Herold fidgeted about, not knowing what to do.

"O sleep, O gentle sleep, Nature's soft nurse..." Booth whispered to himself. Then he turned to his companion. "Get thee to bed, Mister Smith."

Herold moved toward the door.

"See if you can find us a carriage tomorrow. We need to continue our journey unhampered by this little misfortune."

Herold nodded and left. The Englishman and Booth were alone in the room. Booth turned a sharp, bright gaze toward him. Despite his pain, he smiled. Bartlett returned the acknowledgment with the subtlety known only to brothers of a secret society.

* * *

A solemn group of men stood in a small, underground room lit by torch light. They wore dark, unidentifiable uniforms. A large sign hanging on the wall written in intricate calligraphy declared: "Resistance to tyranny is obedience to God."

Among the shadowed faces were Bill Andrews, the Englishman Bartlett, several Union government officials, Confederates leaders. They all wore large badges over their hearts designed with a Maltese Cross inside an eight-pointed star contained within a golden circle. Wearing a similar uniform, Booth made his way through the solemn group. The men began the performance of a secret ritual.

"If you go to the east, I will go the west. Let there be no strife between mine and thine, for we be brethren."

A flag of red and white stripes, with eleven stars in a field of blue dominated the room. Embroidered in the center of the stripes were the initials K. G. C.

Booth watched himself move with the procession through the misty shadows of his dream.

Suddenly, he was walking into the State Box at Ford's Theater. The sound of the ritual chants turned into the cadence of a pounding heartbeat.

His hand rose in front of his face holding a pistol. As the pistol was pointed, Lincoln's head began to turn around, sensing Booth's presence.

The gun fired.

In slow motion, Booth saw himself jump onto the stage.

The words "Sic semper tyrannis!" echoed throughout the theater, as though far away. The sound of his rapid heartbeats turned into galloping hooves and the heavy rasp of a horse's panting.

Booth's feverish mind then saw another unfocused image. A man stood alone on stage, surrounded by colored lights. Dressed as Brutus, Booth saw himself in the midst of a soliloquy.

"Hear me for my cause, and be silent that you may hear. Believe me for mine honor, and have respect to mine honor, that you may believe. Censure me in your wisdom, and awake your senses, that you may be the better judge!"

The faces of a fascinated audience filled his vision.

"If there be any in this assembly, any dear friend of Caesar's, to him I say that Brutus' love..."

He was suddenly in the air, jumping from the railing. A grunt of pain echoed across the stage.

With a jolt, he woke up from his nightmare, his face covered with sweat and twisted in a grimace of agony and regret.

His attention was captured by an early morning sun spreading peaceful pastel colors into the room. He looked out the window toward the lush and peaceful countryside. The tranquillity of life made itself known to him — a contentment that he would never know again.

The sweet harmony of morning birds blended with slow moving clouds and a soft blessing descended upon all living things in his sight...except for him. He was exempted. The curse had begun.

Beneath his window, the Englishman sat on the front porch, fashioning a crude crutch with the skill of long practice. In the kitchen, Mrs. Mudd was preparing breakfast, placing it on a tray to bring up to her wounded guest. In the distance, on the path winding past the home, Herold was returning from town.

Booth sat up on the bed and readied to shave. He looked into a small mirror propped on a bedside table as he shaved off his trademark mustache. He then proceeded to clip his black curls short, transforming the romantic young actor that he was twenty-four hours ago into a gaunt and haunted man. He pulled a black suit out of his bag.

Herold dismounted and tied his horse to a railing on the front porch. The Englishman interrupted his meticulous work and looked up at him inquisitively.

"Everyone in town is needing their carriage. It's Easter Sunday! There are none available."

"What other options have you?" Bartlett asked.

"Maybe the doctor knows someone..."

"Dr. Mudd went to Bryantown to see a patient."

Herold looked out at the countryside glowing in a golden hallow of morning sun, and tried to calm his nerves.

"Perhaps you ought to saddle your friend's horse," the Englishman suggested with the authority of a field commander whose intuitions on such matters were at their prime.

"But the doctor said he couldn't ride..."

"I think your friend will take his chances."

Herold hurried into the house, as though he'd received warning of a coming storm. Mrs. Mudd was just about to go upstairs with a tray of food.

"Don't disturb yourself, ma'am. I'll take it up to him."

"Why, it's no bother at all. I'd..."

Herold nearly tore the tray out of her hand. "Allow me."

He hurried upstairs with the tray as the woman reacted in shock at his uncouth behavior. Herold knocked at the door, nervous energy coursing through his body.

"Enter!"

Herold opened the door but stopped in the doorway, stunned by what he saw. Booth's appearance was greatly altered from cutting off his famous wavy black hair and mustache.

"What the hell are you staring at?"

"You look so..."

"Different?"

"Yeah."

"That's the idea."

"I brought you some breakfast."

"I can't eat! Find me some brandy. Did you find a carriage?"

"No, I..."

"Then steal one!"

"It's Easter Sunday."

"What?" Booth cried out incredulously, with a sharp twinge of guilt shooting through him in light of this holy day.

"They're all being used."

Booth shook his head and touched his broken leg, resigning himself to the pain he would have to endure. "Then ready my horse."

Herold moved into the hallway. "Herold! Don't forget the brandy," he said in a gentler tone. "I need it for the pain."

A glimmer of sympathy sparkled in Herold's eyes as he nod-ded with understanding. His nerves were as mangled as the actor's leg. Booth turned back to the window and sadly eyed the beautiful spring morning. Its peace and harmony clashed dramatically with the extreme tension of his situation. He snapped out of his reverie and began to dress in the Confederate uniform.

Footsteps on the stairway brought out Mrs. Mudd from the kitchen. She was astounded to find Herold helping Booth down the stairs.

"Careful, Herold," Booth said with a grimace. "I don't want to break the other one."

"What in Heaven's name are you doing?" Mrs. Mudd demanded.

"We must be on our way, my dear lady. Pressing business awaits us."

"But you…"

"Please extend to your husband our warmest appreciation for the trouble we have caused him. You have been most hospitable."

They came to the bottom of the stairs. She was surprised by Booth's change of appearance, but more concerned about his terri-ble wound.

"Won't you stay for lunch?"

"Some other time perhaps, if we come this way again."

She watched them leave the house. A sudden apprehension took hold of her.

"Farewell, Mrs. Mudd," Booth said without turning back as he limped away.

The Englishman offered the crutch to Booth as Herold hurried to the horses. The two men exchanged intense, silent looks, speak-ing to each other without words. Herold returned with the horses and they helped Booth onto his mount. Booth grasped Bartlett's forearm and quoted the bard's heartfelt lines.

"Forever, and forever, farewell. If we do not meet again, why then this parting was well made."

Herold suddenly sat up in his saddle, seeing something in the distance.

"Mister Booth!" he said with alarm.

Booth glared at him, angered at his slip of the tongue. He looked in the direction in which Herold was pointing. In the distance, Dr. Mudd was whipping his horse into a frenetic gallop, sending the little carriage bouncing dangerously along the road.

Booth waved good-bye to Mrs. Mudd with a veneer of calm and trotted off toward the woods. Herold hurried after him. Seeing her husband approach, Mrs. Mudd ran to the gate in a state of growing agitation. The Englishman watched the scene serenely, satisfied with the way things were going, and then returned into the house knowing that his work was done.

Dr. Mudd pulled his carriage up to the gate.

"Martha!"

Mrs. Mudd ran breathlessly toward him.

"Martha! The President's been assassinated!"

She stumbled to the carriage, eyes filled with horror.

"Our guests have just left in a big hurry...Oh Sam! What have we done?"

Trembling with foreboding, Dr. Mudd desperately embraced his wife.

* * *

Booth and Herold galloped down a narrow path. A small troop of soldiers suddenly appeared ahead of them and they frantically dashed off into another direction. Further down the path, another troop was coming through the underbrush. The two men jerked their horses toward another pathway. They raced down the dirt road, looking back to see if the soldiers had spotted them.

"I hear horses ahead of us! Holy Christ, we're surrounded!" Herold cried out. "This way!"

They crashed into the woods, tearing through thorns and branches. Another regiment came upon the path as they disappeared. They slowly made their way through the dense forest. The peaceful sounds of the forest surrounded them as they forged a passage through the thicket, a shocking contrast to the terror still thundering in their ears.

They came upon swampland extending indefinitely through the quiet wilderness. Mosquitoes swarmed around them. They stopped as their horses began to sink in the thick mud.

"We're gonna be eaten alive!"

"Maybe we can circle this swamp down to the right," Booth advised as he strained to see through the thick brush.

They moved on, fighting mosquitoes and thorns. The mud became thicker and more treacherous. Booth's horse stepped into quicksand.

"Herold! I'm stuck!"

Herold couldn't manage to turn his horse around in the thick growth.

"Hurry! I'm sinking!"

Herold jumped off his horse and wallowed in the mud toward Booth.

"Careful! Don't come too close or you'll get stuck!"

Herold held onto a tree limb as Booth threw him the reins. After a difficult struggle, Herold pulled the horse out of the mud. He sat back against a tree, exhausted.

"How in hell are we gonna get outta here?"

"Keep moving. Just keep moving."

They continued on. All around them swampland extended as far as they could see.

The sun began to set. The two men were utterly lost in bogs. Not a sign of civilization anywhere. Booth pulled the reins in and took out a bottle of brandy. Herold nursed the cuts on his legs from thorns and bushes.

"We should stop before the sun goes down," Booth said. "Otherwise we're going to find ourselves in the middle of this swamp with no way out."

Herold looked at the barren countryside, about to weep at the thought of spending the night here.

"Tell me, Herold. Do you know your geography?"

"I can tell which way is north when the stars come out."

"I'm referring to your knowledge of the world."

"I don't understand."

"I was thinking about Calcutta. I don't think we'll have to worry about swamps and mosquitoes in Calcutta."

"Don't think I know the place, Mister Booth."

"That's our destination, our port of call. Our exile."

"Is it far from London?"

"London? Why, it's on the other side of the world from London."

"How can that be, Mister Booth?" Herold asked, confused. "Aren't we being taken to England?"

"In order to reach the trade route, yes."

"And then what?"

"Then on to India, or perhaps Shanghai."

"There ain't too many Americans in them parts, is there?"

"We might come across a few Confederates. Judah Benjamin, the Secretary of State, is out there somewhere."

They rode on, watching the sun vanish behind the scraggly mass of trees.

"I ain't never felt so lonely, Mister Booth."

Booth looked at him with compassion. He offered him the brandy bottle. Herold refused it.

"Come, it'll warm you up. Make you imagine you're by a cozy fireplace." Herold hesitated. Booth smiled at him for the first time. Herold took the bottle and drank.

"You'll not find a soul on this earth more alone than you and I tonight. We've been tossed into the winds of Fate, we've played our parts, and there are no more lines to read. You know, Herold, all the great men I've played, those words of truth and honor and sacrifice...They were all a rehearsal. I was being trained, cultivated by Destiny to play this necessary, inevitable part."

He looked up at the dying colors in the sky and projected dramatically for the swamp creatures to hear.

"My fate cries out, and makes each petty artery in this body as hardy as the Nemean lion's nerve!"

He winced in pain from the sudden movement of his arm, automatically performing the words for an audience. He closed his eyes and snickered desperately at the wretchedness into which he had fallen.

A rustle was heard nearby. Booth pulled out his pistol. The sound in the bushes grew louder.

"Help me out of my saddle!" he whispered urgently to his companion.

Herold quickly helped Booth off the horse. He moaned as they knelt down in the bushes.

"What is it? Soldiers?" Herold whimpered.

A silhouette suddenly appeared among the trees. In the red light of the setting sun, the figure seemed monstrous, the vision of some vengeful ghost searching for its tormentors.

"What the hell is it?"

"There's only one of them, whatever it is," Booth responded as he put back his pistol in its holster.

He pulled out a knife as the silhouette approached. The men held their breath. Footsteps approached. A black man appeared in the dim light. He gasped at the sight of the two crouching silhouettes. Booth raised his knife.

"Who are you?" Booth called out, looking like a demon as the pale moonlight sparkled on his sharp blade.

"Swann. Oswald Swann, sir," the man cried out, terrified.

"What are you doing out here?"

"I live nearby," he answered in a trembling voice.

"In the swamps?" Booth asked suspiciously.

"I got no place else to go. If Colonel Cox finds me, he'll hang me for sure."

"Who's Colonel Cox?"

"My master. I...I ran away a couple weeks ago."

Booth studied the man with the skills of an astute observer. Herold kept his gun pointed at him.

"Put that down, Herold," Booth finally said. "Mister Swann isn't going to hurt anyone. Come over here, Mister Swann."

The frightened man approached. He was both jubilant and terrorized to see other humans after his long solitude.

"Sit down, won't you?" Booth said gallantly as he put his knife away.

Swann sat in the tiny clearing and Booth offered him the

brandy bottle. Swann hesitated and finally took it with gratitude.

"The war's over, Mister Swann. You're a free man."

Swann handed the bottle back to him, astounded. His eyes filled with tears.

"Hallelujah! Hallelujah! God bless that good Mister Lincoln."

Swann took notice of the men's cold reactions to his words.

"Where does Colonel Cox live?" Booth asked.

"A couple miles from here."

"Near the Potomac river?"

"Yessuh."

"Can you take us there? We're lost. We'll pay you for your trouble."

"I can't do that, sir!" the man said in horror.

"Let's hurry," Booth insisted as he picked up his bags.

"You ain't gonna turn me in, is you?"

"You have my word, Mister Swann. No one is your master now, save the Almighty."

The men gathered their things and moved out, cutting their way through the thick foliage.

After a short while, they spotted the lights of a large mansion. They came to the edge of the woods.

"I can't take you no further."

"I'll give you ten dollars if you go find Colonel Cox and bring him here," Booth told him.

"I can't do that!" Swann responded in terror.

"You'd better!" Herold said with his hand on his gun.

"We need your help badly, Mister Swann. Our lives are in your hands."

Swann hesitated. Booth pulled out a silver star and handed it to the shivering man.

"You show him this. He won't lay a hand on you."

Swann looked at the strange symbol as though it was some magical talisman. Booth took out a large roll of money and gave him a few bills. Swann accepted them gratefully, took a deep breath, and headed for the house.

Booth and Herold waited silently in the darkness.

"I don't trust him. He might just take off with the money."

"He's a decent man. He won't leave us out here, I'll wager on it."

The moon rose high into the sky. Booth waited patiently as Herold fidgeted nervously. A lantern appeared from the mansion. Two silhouettes approached them — an aristocratic Southern officer, Colonel Cox, and his brother Thomas Jones.

Colonel Cox put out his hand in friendship.

"I don't know what your mission is, brother, but I'm honored to be of assistance." The Colonel shook Booth's hand and returned the star to him.

"This is Thomas Jones, my foster brother. He's the chief agent of the underground here in Maryland."

Booth acknowledged him as did Herold.

"We must get to the Potomac," the actor said urgently.

"The yanks have confiscated all the boats. It'll take some doing to find one," the colonel stated with concern.

"How long will that take, Colonel?"

"A few days, maybe. I'm afraid you'll have to stay in the woods. Soldiers are always comin' round here. I'll provide you with food and blankets. Tom will bring you some supper. Here, you'd better keep the lantern."

He handed the lantern to Herold. They turned to head back up to the house.

"Colonel," Booth called out, "Where's Mister Swann?"

"Who?"

"Your negro."

"Oh, you won't be seein' him again."

He smiled an evil grin and walked off. Booth's eyes darkened as a feeling of expanding sorrow flood his heart. His act was destroying other lives in its wake.

They returned into the woods and settled in a small clearing. Herold helped Booth off his horse. They sat against a tree, ragged and tired. Booth offered brandy to his companion who took a long swig. The gloomy actor lay back on the ground and looked up through the trees at the full moon. He contemplated it as it peeked out mysteriously from the clouds.

An image formed itself in his feverish mind.

A dark stage. A packed theater. His majestic and melancholic brother, Edwin Booth dressed as Marc Antony. Edwin moved through the set—ruins bathed in moonlight. Every gesture, every muscle movement reflected a magnificent presence, filled with elegance and power. Then he spoke, in words couched in a rich baritone voice full of emotion.

"This was the noblest Roman of them all. All the conspirators save only he did that they did in envy of great Caesar;

He, only in a general honest thought

And common good to all, made one of them.

His life was gentle, and the elements so mixed in him

that Nature might stand up and say to all the world,

'This was a man!'"

In the humid swampland, John Booth wept at his fall from grace. He had imagined himself the "noblest of them all" and now was forsaken as the vilest of criminals.

Another image filled Booth's inner sight as he lay in the damp soil. The sounds of a passionate argument filled ears. He found himself in Edwin's lavish living room. John smashed his fist on a table in anger. Edwin leaned calmly on a marble mantle over a large fireplace. As always, he was restrained and stoic.

"Lincoln's election forced the war!" John cried out. "Edwin, in a foreign war I would also say 'country, right or wrong.' But in a struggle such as this one, where brother tries to pierce his brother's heart, for God's sake choose the right side! When a country spurns justice, she forfeits the allegiance of every honest man, and should leave him unbound by any loyalty whatsoever to act as his conscience may approve!"

"The President's policy is..." Edwin interjected.

"Lincoln's policy is only preparing the way for total annihilation! The South is not, nor ever has been, fighting for the continuance of slavery. The first battle at Bull Run did away with that idea. The Confederate causes for war are as noble as those that urged our fathers on. Even if we allowed that they were wrong at the beginning, cruelty and injustice have made the wrong become the right!"

Edwin moved to the window, and studied the rainstorm raging among the trees.

John came up behind him, trembling with emotion.

"When I aided in the capture and execution of John Brown, I was proud of my little part in the drama, because I deemed it my duty, and that I was helping our country to perform an act of justice. But what was a crime in poor John Brown is now considered as the greatest and only virtue of the whole Republican party!"

"You don't know what you're saying, John," Edwin muttered grimly.

"What a strange transmigration!" John cried out passionately as he stormed around the room. "Vice becomes virtue simply because more people indulge in it! I thought then, as I do now, that the Abolitionists were the only traitors in the land, and that the entire party deserved the same fate as old John Brown!"

Edwin turned around, furious. "That's enough!"

"Not because they want to abolish slavery," John continued unabated, "but on account of the means they have used to effect that abolition. If Brown were living, I doubt whether he would set slavery against the Union.

"Edwin, most or nearly all the North openly curse the Union if the South is to return and retain a single right guaranteed to them by every tie which we once revered as sacred. What choice can the South make? It's either extermination or slavery!"

John returned to his brother's side, pleading for his understanding

"Oh, Edwin, if you had known Her as I have! You always toured the East with father while I was playing the houses in Richmond, Atlanta, Charleston..."

"Then why did you not go out onto the battlefield?"

John looked at him sadly, eyes sparkling with despair.

"I gave my word four years ago to our mother, while she was grieving over the execution of cousin Harry, that I would not take part in the fighting. I am bound by that promise. But I do not have to stand on a battlefield to see the effects and realities of this horrid war in every state, every city...I know you would think like me if you could witness the rape of that gentle culture I have loved."

Edwin turned away from him and stared out the window with dark intensity.

"And you would pray the Almighty to create a sense of right

and justice in the northern mind and dry up the sea of blood between us!" John said in a desperate whisper.

Weary and distressed, he moved away from his brother.

"This is the end of constitutional America. I have no more country. She is approaching her doom. Lincoln should be shot! I hope someone kills him."

Edwin turned around, stunned.

"You don't mean that, Johnny...You don't really mean that."

"With all my heart."

"How my brother can vilify his soul with such evil thoughts...such horrendous wrath..."

He cut himself off and seemed to drift away on a wave of profound melancholy. Words fell from his mouth, rising from the mists of his memories.

"Give me that man that is not passion's slave and I will wear him in my heart's core, aye, in my heart of hearts..."

He looked over toward his younger brother who stood across the room from him and shook his head.

"When you talk like that, you're no longer my little brother."

"I am a patriot!" John shouted, out of control with rage.

"Thou shalt not kill!" Edwin thundered back.

"What empty words at the climax of this perverse fratricide!"

They stared each other down. Finally, Edwin's features softened into a grimace of great sadness.

"See what it has made of us, Johnny..."

"Too much has been destroyed, too many good men killed, to indulge in trivial sentimentality," John said coldly.

Edwin's eyes glazed with anger.

"Get out of my house! You are no longer welcomed here!"

The two brothers stared at each other intensely. Then John

grabbed his hat and left.

Tears rolled down Booth's muddy cheeks as his memories of the life he had given up fell upon him like a deadly tidal wave.

The roar and applause of an ecstatic audience exploded in his ears as he saw himself with his brother Edwin, dressed as Marc Antony and himself as Brutus, step before a cast in Roman costume. Side by side, they bowed gracefully. The famous brothers smiled at each other, grasped arms, and bowed again and again.

The applause faded as Booth felt the cold of night pull him back to the wretchedness of his situation. He closed his eyes, frantically seeking a peaceful place in the depths of his soul.

Another image filled his mind's eye. A golden spring day. A large, aging man, the great Junius Brutus Booth, and a little boy walked together through the lush foliage.

The father and son shared quietly the joy of exploring Nature's beauty on this peaceful day. They came to an isolated stream and sat under a tree. The little boy with the large brown eyes settled on his father's lap.

Looking out across the ravishing countryside, the father's raspy, dramatic voice echoed in the meadow as he shared his own poetry with his son.

"*He prayeth well who loveth well,*
Both man and bird and beast.
He prayeth best who lovest best,
All things both great and small.
And the dear God who loveth us,
He made and loveth all."

Junius Brutus Booth, the great tragedian, looked down at his young son and caressed his head.

"I wrote that poem for you, Johnny..."

He kissed him on the forehead. They contemplated the tranquil scene around them, happy and serene.

In the dark swampland, John Wilkes Booth wept like a baby.

FOUR

A bright sun shimmered through the trees. Thomas Jones made his way through thick woods, carrying a basket of food and newspapers.

He came upon the small clearing where Booth and Herold hid. Herold was washing his face in a stream. Booth sat against a tree, writing in a little diary notebook.

"Good day, Thomas. Found anything?" Booth asked.

"No luck yet. But the organization is aware of the situation. I'm sure you'll have a boat by tomorrow."

"Tomorrow?" Herold said in terror.

"I've heard tell that several regiments are headed this way."

He put down the food basket and handed the newspaper to Booth who took them avidly. But this features quickly froze in shock as he saw the large, bold headlines: "Crazed Actor" — "Megalomaniac" — "Lone Killer."

Booth's mouth dropped open in utter stupefaction.

"We'll have you out of here in time," Jones said to ease the tension. "A brother is going to send them chasing into Saint Mary's County. It's been arranged for Tom Harbin, my brother-in-law, to meet you downriver and help you across to the Virginia side. He'll put you in touch with Mrs. Quesenberry who'll take you to Dr. Stuart. From there, you'll be taken across Port Conway to the Appahannock River. Captain Jett will meet you at the ferry."

Booth seemed to be in a catatonic state. Jones and Herold grew increasingly disturbed by his strange condition.

"I'll...I'll be back around sunset with more provisions."

Booth paid no attention to his departure. Herold approached the ghostly pale man, worried. The newspapers slipped out of the actor's hands. He stood up and, leaning on his crutch, walked blindly to the stream. He fell to his knees with a grimace of pain, and plunged his head in the water. Then he lay on his back and stared at the sky with a look of horror in his eyes.

Herold didn't dare make a noise and finally went to sit against a tree, shaken by the trauma that had overtaken his companion.

Booth felt light-headed. An intense dizziness swept over him. He realized that he was about to lose consciousness from the pain and lack of sleep. As he felt himself loosen his grip from the confines of his body, a flood of images crashed upon him. He was aware that he was being pulled out to sea.

He heard a distant voice calling to him as images in his mind became more real than his surroundings. It was David Herold.

"Mister Booth, are you all right?"

But it was too late. He was already on his way toward an unconsciousness that sent him far into his inner world.

He heard an angelic sound. As it became clearer, he recognized the soft singing of a little girl playing by herself on a sunny day. The innocent melody became clearer and he recognized the beloved voice of his daughter, Ogarita.

"Little Rita..." he heard himself say from the very core of his soul.

An image came into focus, bathed in the golden light of a peaceful spring day. A four-year-old girl with coal black locks and marble white skin was dancing on the porch of a country home. She turned around and saw her daddy looking at her through the window. A great radiant smile lit her face. It seemed brighter than the sun. She waved a little chubby hand and went back to her singing with added enthusiasm, expressing the joy of witnessing her father's infinite love for her.

An aroma of mouth-watering food filled the air and mixed with the child's gentle song. In the kitchen, Izola D'Arcy was preparing a family meal. He turned around and caught sight of the silhouette of the other love of his life. She felt his gaze and turned large, Spanish eyes upon him. She blew him a kiss as she stirred the food she was preparing with such affection.

He had known many women of all types in his travels and theatrical triumphs. They threw themselves at him as though he were some incarnate god. When the footlights came on and he stepped onto the stage, he felt himself as such. Always sharply dressed in striking black that highlighted his pale angular face and its intense dark eyes, he was an irresistible sight to the women who crowded around the matinee idol and seemed to lose all sense of the morals of the day.

He had taken advantage of his flock of admirers many times, especially his leading ladies who had fallen madly in love with him. There was not another actor in his generation who could match his animal magnetism and virile presence. He carried with him the fury and tempest of his father's universally acclaimed talents. They were packaged in a body that was the envy of every man and the delight of every woman.

John enjoyed his bohemian life and the fortune he was making each week spouting Shakespearean poetry to thrilled audiences. His acting skills were matched by athletic ones that he used to the hilt, jumping onto the stage from ten foot platforms, and dueling with ferocity. He turned the ancient plays into dynamic events that astonished crowds hungry for distraction. And when the grease-paint was taken off and the costumes removed, he performed other feats with the women who surrounded him.

He had stolen the hearts of countless young actresses and wealthy women from the good families of Richmond, Boston, and Philadelphia. It was too easy for him and he paid little attention to the emotional carnage he left behind. Among his forlorn lovers were senators' daughters who expected to marry the handsomest man in America. None had tamed him. Until he met Izola Mills D'Arcy.

Izola's powerful personality matched his passionate energies. Her beauty melted his soul and body every time he gazed upon her. She had instantly given up her theatrical career when their professional relationship had turned to romance, even though she knew that he would never be faithful to her in body. But they were both certain that their souls were from all eternity meant to be united.

Now she made a home for him and gave him a little girl who charmed him as much as her mother did. She had no intention of slowing down his meteoric career and his triumphs across the land. Izola understood that the roar of the crowd and the rise of the curtain could not compete in the long run with the peace and contentment that their home provided for his restless soul.

John moved into the kitchen and put his arms around her waist. He pressed his cheek against her thick, fragrant hair and breathed deeply the scent of his beloved. This was heaven for a man whose spirit seemed forever on fire. Even without the horror of the war between the states, the tumultuous life of the theater and the instability of his father's ways had created a man who needed to find a peaceful oasis in a world of noise and madness.

Izola and little Rita gave him all that he needed to fulfill his life. The future glories on stage that awaited him, the certainty of wealth and fame were secondary to the indescribable sweetness of these moments with his secret family. John didn't want his audiences to know that he was at heart an ordinary family man who relished the simple joys of life and found them to be his greatest treasures. The persona he had created so diligently was designed to live up to the mighty Booth name, and he had to remain single and aloof—unapproachable even. This was the way of the actor, forever changing faces and costumes, moving from one life to the other, delighting audiences with death scenes, words of wisdom, passionate kisses.

Behind all of that bright fanfare and melodrama was the youth who had grown up in the heart of nature on his father's Baltimore farm. He could not forget the true pleasures of life—the warmth of sunshine, a quiet afternoon, butterflies alighting on lush and brightly colored flowers. This was the real glory of life and he knew it, even while taking his tenth curtain call and basking in the deafening applause of admirers. His father had taught him where true meaning was to be found even though the old man had failed to discover his own peace of mind. John expected to conquer that treasure, just as he had conquered audiences in the North and South alike.

Now in this kitchen filled with delicious aromas, in the company of a woman of unbridled passion and loyalty and the sweet sound of a little girl whom he loved more than life itself, John Booth had come upon the peace that had eluded his father and brothers. And he still had his whole life before him. He knew that the day would come when he would grow weary of the city lights and the frenzied atmosphere of the theater, and even of the women who knocked on his dressing room door. Then he would come home once and for all, never to leave again.

As he kissed his beloved's cheek and tightened his arms around her, he felt a twinge of pain cut into his chest, interfering with the contentment that was within his reach. The war had changed everything and there could be no home and no peace until the catastrophe that had destroyed his country was concluded. He leaned forward and blended his lips with hers.

* * *

Carrying lanterns covered by oilcloths, Booth and Herold followed Thomas Jones through the underbrush along the banks of the river.

Jones led them to a boat hidden at the edge of the water. He showed Booth the course to steer and handed him a compass. The men helped Booth into the boat and Herold took hold of the oars.

Thomas Jones embraced both of them and pushed the boat out into the river.

For a while, they floated down the quiet, moonlit river. Booth scribbled madly in a makeshift diary, mumbling to himself. Herold watched him sadly.

"After being hunted like a dog through swamps and woods, I am here in despair. And why? For doing what Brutus was honored for. For doing what made William Tell a hero."

The sound of crickets and of the oars softly pushing through the water contrasted sharply with the men's tension. Booth continued to write relentlessly.

"And yet I, for striking down a greater tyrant than they ever knew, am looked upon as a common cut-throat. My action was purer than either of theirs. One hoped to be great. The other had not only his country's, but his own wrongs to avenge. I struck for my country and that alone."

In the distance, along the banks, lights moved through the woods. Herold watched their pursuers coming dangerously close. Booth was oblivious to his surroundings.

"A country that groaned beneath this tyranny and prayed for this end, and yet, now behold the cold hand they extend to me. God cannot pardon me if I have done wrong!"

Herold blew out the lantern, snapping Booth out of his feverish reflections. The boat glided along in darkness as distant voices yelling orders became distinguishable on the banks of the river.

Booth and Herold crouched down in the boat. The ghostly shadows of soldiers galloped near the banks.

Suddenly, the boat hit a rock with a loud crash. Booth pushed Herold further down into the boat. Several soldiers looked out at the river.

Finally, they moved on. Booth looked up, lit the lantern and returned to his writing.

"The little, the very little I left behind to clear my name, the government will not allow to be printed. So ends all...For my country I have given up all that makes life sweet and holy; brought misery on my family, and now know that there is no pardon in the Heavens for me since man condemns me so."

Another boat appeared ahead of them. Herold blew out the lantern and cocked his gun. The two boats almost crashed into each other. An old farmer was steering the other craft.

"Hey! Light your damn lantern! I almost ran into you."

"Our lantern fell overboard," Herold said as calmly as he could.

"Well, be careful. There's a lot a rocks round here."

He held up another lantern. "Here, catch. I got two of them."

He tossed the lantern toward them. Herold caught it and smiled at him gratefully.

"Very kind of you, friend," Booth said. "God bless you."

The man waved and disappeared in the obscurity. The boat glided on. Booth lit the lantern and poured out his dark thoughts on the crumpled paper.

"Though I have a great desire and almost a mind to return to Washington, and in a measure, clear my name—which I feel I can do—I do not repent the blow I struck. I may before my God, but not to man. I think I have done well.

"I am abandoned, with the curse of Cain upon me, when if the world knew my heart, that one blow would have made me great, though I desire no greatness."

A dog barked at them from the bank. Herold looked over, nervous. Booth continued his mutterings, oblivious of the dangers around them.

"Who can read this fate? God's will be done. I have too great a soul to die like a criminal. Oh, may He spare me that, and let me die bravely."

Herold stared up at the stars, seeking peace for himself and his companion.

"I bless the entire world," Booth continued. "I have never hated nor wronged anyone. This deed was not a wrong, unless God deems it so. And it is with him to damn or bless me. I do not wish to shed a drop of blood, but I must fight the course. 'Tis all that is left me."

The boat drifted off into the night.

The sun was just rising over the horizon, sending streaks of gold and pink across the landscape as the boat approached a small beach. Booth and Herold were exhausted. They came ashore with difficulty.

Herold stretched as Booth scanned the countryside. He took a few deep breaths to revive himself. Herold helped him up the hill leading into the woods.

A man waved at them from the thicket. He had been waiting for them for several hours. They greeted each other somberly at the edge of the woods and headed off to the next leg of their escape.

* * *

A regiment of sixteen soldiers pulled up in front of a roadside tavern. Dust-covered and mud-splattered, they eagerly dismounted and entered.

The men sat at the tables as two officers and a man in civilian clothes stepped up to the bar—Major Doherty, Lieutenant Baker and Everton Conger, a detective.

They sat in silence on the bar stools for a moment, drinking.

"You think we'll get to him first?" Major Doherty wondered.

"For a hundred-thousand dollars worth of reward, we sure as hell are gonna do our damndest," Baker responded.

"What other regiments are in the area?"

"Major O'Beirne is around here somewhere," Conger replied with an edge of concern in his voice.

"We got nothin' to worry about," Baker assured them. "If Booth is in the neighborhood, we'll get to him first."

He swallowed his whiskey and announced with confidence: "My cousin promised me that."

"Your cousin?" the major asked, confused.

"Yeah."

"What the hell are you talking about, Lieutenant?" Conger barked.

"Ever heard of Colonel Baker?"

"Colonel Lafayette Baker?" the detective asked, his eyes widening.

"That's my cousin," the crusty lieutenant stated with pride.

"You're kidding!" Major Doherty shouted out as he slammed his glass on the bar.

"You know me better than that, Major. I'm tellin' ya, my cousin is head of the Secret Service, and we got a deal worked out. If we play our cards right, with a little luck, we'll never have to eat army slop again."

He snickered as he saw the greed twinkling in the eyes of his companions.

"Secretary Stanton wants him alive, right?" Major Doherty asked after a moment.

"Nah. That's for the papers," the detective responded cynically. "He wants a body that will close this case before the country blows up again."

"Well, what the hell are we waiting for?" the major cried out. "Let's get after him!"

He threw a coin on the bar and headed for the door with renewed energy.

"Off your butts, men! We're movin' out!"

Baker smiled at Conger, spit out his tobacco juice, and followed the soldiers out of the saloon.

* * *

Budding cherry blossoms warmed by the morning sun graced the windowsill in the office of the Secretary of War. Edwin Stanton looked through the window, pensively. He turned around abruptly.

"What was that name you mentioned, Colonel Baker?"

An aging warrior with thick silver hair, Colonel Baker sat uncomfortably by Stanton's desk.

"The Knights of the Golden Circle."

Stanton walked over to his desk and picked up a star symbol similar to the one Booth carried with him. He examined it carefully.

"They've held the South together from the beginning, Mister Secretary," the Colonel said solemnly. "My men have been investigating..."

"What makes you think that Northerners are affiliated with them?" Stanton growled, interrupting the officer.

"The Knights are connected to other secret brotherhoods. The Sons of Liberty, the American Legion, the Freemasons...They've got senators, newspaper editors..."

"Do you realize what you're implying, Colonel?"

"I wouldn't waste your time or mine if I didn't have solid facts. These people were responsible for Union defeats. They passed off plans to the other side. They ran secret missions in Canada and have close ties with England. My informants have even dug up some wild scheme to set up an empire in Central America and Mexico in order to strengthen the South."

Stanton paced behind his desk like a caged and raging animal of the wilds.

"You don't really believe that Union politicians are working with them, do you, Colonel?"

"Sir, the anti-reconstructionists are as much against the President's policy as..."

"Where is your proof of this? Where?" Stanton yelled furiously, throwing the star on the desk.

"They number over three hundred thousand, Mister Secretary," the colonel said with hesitation. "Some eighty-five thousand in Illinois, fifty thousand in Indiana, forty thousand in Ohio. Brigadier-General George Bickley, head of the Confederate Secret Service, is said to be their leader."

"Will that be all, Colonel?" Stanton asked abruptly.

Colonel Baker stared at him in shock, and then stood rigidly. He turned to leave.

"Take these toys with you," Stanton ordered, pointing at the emblems.

Red with anger and humiliation, Colonel Baker picked up the symbols, and hurried out of the office. Stanton looked out at the cherry blossoms. His eyes glazed with a terrible tension.

* * *

Booth, Herold, and a guide rode up to a desolate ferry. Herold hurried into the waterside hut where the ferryman was repairing his fishnets. The guide helped Booth off his horse. He sat on a woodpile, weak with pain. Unshaven and covered with mud, he was in a nearly delirious state. The man looked around for soldiers.

Two confederate officers appeared from the woods and approached them quickly. They saluted Booth. One of them turned his horse around and galloped back into the woods, while Captain William Jett stayed with Booth.

Leaving the guide ashore, the three men boarded the large raft used for ferrying. Booth collapsed on the crates.

"Would you happen to have any cigars on you, Captain Jett?" the actor asked with a gallantry that seemed strangely out of place under the circumstances.

"I've got a whole box for you, Mister Booth."

Jett took a box of cigars from his saddlebag and offered one to Booth.

"Thank you, Captain."

Jett offered one to Herold who took it eagerly.

"Call me Bill. This isn't the place for formalities."

"No, that it isn't, Bill," Booth responded, blowing smoke with great pleasure. "No more time for formalities. No more time for lies."

A shiver of pain shot through his body.

"Would you like some brandy, Mister Booth?" Herold asked, observing his condition with compassion.

"My God...I never thought a man could feel so much pain and still hold on to his senses."

Herold handed him a bottle. He drank and then looked down at his left ankle.

"See that lump there, Bill? That's a piece of bone cutting its way into my boot."

He let out a groan. "Damn it! When I played Macbeth, I would make my entrance by jumping off a twelve foot ledge. I must have done it a hundred times. And never a bruise. Not once."

"We're going to get you to your destination, Mister Booth," Jett said with passion, "and this nightmare will be over soon."

"Clean, warm sheets, a soft mattress...They'd better have soft mattresses on board, Captain Jett. My kingdom for a mattress!"

He laughed in desperation.

"Maybe you should try to get some sleep," Jett suggested.

"With sixteen hundred bloodthirsty men on my trail? I knew sleep would not favor me for a long while when I loaded that pistol. No, I don't want to sleep. If I'm caught, I want to see them coming."

Herold tightened his grip on his carbine, shuddering. Booth looked over at him, disgusted by his cowardice.

"Cowards die many times before their deaths; the valiant never taste of death but once," he said proudly.

He raised the bottle as though toasting the poet whose words he knew so well, and drank. His eyes bloodshot and glazed, on the edge of complete exhaustion, he stared off into running waters, forgetting his companions.

Hazy images filled his mind, giving him a brief escape from his agonizing situation.

Some fifteen actors and actresses sat at a table in a fancy restaurant, all in a joyful mood. Dressed in fine clothing, Booth was seated next to a beautiful young lady.

John Ford, the theater manager, tapped his knife on his wine-glass and rose at the head of the table.

"Your attention please, dear friends. Cassius, will you take your hands off of Calpurnia, and pay attention. It's my turn to make a speech. At least I won't have to pay a fortune to have this one presented."

The actors laughed merrily.

"Let us toast the man who is proving himself to be the greatest actor of his time," Ford continued. Booth acknowledged the compliment with a slight bow.

"His Macbeth and Richard the Third are different from any other I have ever witnessed. His Raphael in "The Marble Heart" is simply matchless. When we played Boston, he made the greatest success of any actor I've ever had the pleasure to engage. People waited in crowds after the performance to catch a glimpse of him as he left the theater."

Ford raised his glass. The entire group did the same.

"To the handsomest man in America, our beloved friend, John Booth."

Booth snapped out of his recollection. He noticed Jett and Herold staring at him with eyes filled with worry. He took a swig of brandy to ease the pain. This time, it wasn't for the broken bone.

* * *

Major O'Beirne, a dignified and highly respected soldier, and his officers huddled around a map. They stood in the area where Thomas Jones had hidden the boat.

A messenger galloped up to the group. He hurried to the Major.

"Major O'Beirne, I have a wire from Washington, sir."

The officer read it. He looked at his officers, stunned.

"We've been ordered to discontinue the expedition and stay this side of the Potomac."

The officers burst out in exclamations of shock and surprise.

"We're right behind him!" one of them said angrily. "What the hell are they doing?"

"There's a small regiment taking over from here," the major stated, looking at the message.

"That's insane! We've tracked them down all the way!"

"Those are the orders, Lieutenant. From high command. I don't have any questions. Do you?"

"No sir," the man said, lowering his eyes.

"Let's go home, men!" Major O'Beirne announced loudly.

They mounted and the regiment rode away from the river.

Standing protectively in front of their home, farmer Garrett and his two sons watched three men ride up to their property. Jett dismounted and walked up to them.

"Good afternoon, sir. My name is Bill Jett. I'm a captain in the Confederate army. My friends are trying to get back down South. Henry here as been wounded. I wonder if you'd be good enough to put them up for the night. I'll come and get them early in the morning."

"Y'all soldiers?" the farmer asked.

"Yes, sir. Heading home," Booth answered with a smile.

"Where was you wounded at?"

"A skirmish outside of Richmond. We're just about all that's left of our regiment."

"Where's your home?"

"Georgia, sir."

Garrett studied them suspiciously.

"My home's always been open to Southerners. You boys come on in and make yourselves comfortable. Take care of their horses, son."

"That's mighty kind of you, sir," Booth said with gratitude.

Herold dismounted and helped Booth down. The son took hold of their horses.

"I'll be back in the morning," Jett whispered to Booth. "Try to get some rest. You've got a long journey ahead of you. If there's any trouble, Boyd will come to warn you."

"Boyd? John Boyd is out here?" Booth asked in surprise.

"He's with Mosby's command."

Booth smiled with new confidence.

"They won't start back until you're safely out of the area."

They shook hands and Jett galloped off. Booth and Herold walked toward the house. Booth gave his companion a warm tap on the shoulder as Garrett led them into his home.

"We were just sittin' down to dinner. Would you care to join us?"

"I haven't seen good Southern cooking for a long time."

"It's nothin' fancy, mind you."

They entered the house as the family gathered around the strangers with a mixture of curiosity and fear.

FIVE

A blood-red sun slowly vanished behind the hills. Lieutenant Baker and his men burst into a dark saloon. Exhausted, his men fell into chairs, hardly able to keep their eyes open.

"Get some whiskey in your stomachs, boys. You gotta stay awake," Baker shouted out to his men as he leaned against the bar with Conger and Major Doherty.

"They gotta get some sleep, Lieutenant. We been ridin' for two days," Conger observed.

"Major O'Beirne was hot on Booth's tail when my cousin called him off. We'd better find him soon or people are gonna wonder what the hell is going on."

"He can't be very far. Somebody must have seen him around here."

The bartender approached them and leaned forward.

"There's a Confederate captain upstairs. He might be able to help you," he whispered.

"What would he know?" Baker muttered.

"He seemed awful excited about somethin' when he brought his lady-friend in here."

Baker looked at the others.

"It's worth a try..."

"Shall I take some of the boys up there?" Major Doherty suggested, tightening his gloves around his fingers.

"Yeah, why don't you. It could be entertaining if nothin' else," Baker added.

"Room thirteen," the bartender said with a sadistic grin.

Major Doherty turned to the soldiers.

"Curtis! Dobson! Burke! Come with me."

Three big men followed him up the stairs. The steps creaked under their weight. Doherty signaled for the men to move quietly. They came to the top of the stairs and slowly walked down the corridor. They approached room thirteen. Doherty listened at the door. The sound of slight moans could be heard from within. Doherty smiled. He tried the doorknob. It was not locked.

The soldiers burst into the room. Jett jumped up, terrified. A partly undressed woman in the bed next to him screamed in terror. Jett dashed for the window but the men grabbed him. They threw him back toward the bed as the woman huddled in the corner.

Major Doherty watched on while the soldiers savagely beat Jett.

"That's enough. He's gotta be able to talk."

They dragged him out of the room. Major Doherty looked at the woman and snickered as she shivered with fear.

The men carried Jett down the stairs and brought him to Baker. The other soldiers hardly paid attention as they fell asleep at the tables. Baker grabbed Jett by the hair.

"Where's John Wilkes Booth?"

"I don't know..."

Baker kneed him in the groin, then punched him in the face with full force.

"Don't give me that, reb! Where is he?"

Jett refused to answer.

"These boys are gonna smear you all over the room if you don't talk!"

"I told you, I don't know."

"We ain't playin' games, boy!"

Baker cracked him across the face. Jett stood helplessly in front of him, wavering. Baker pulled out a knife.

"I'm gonna skin you, boy! I swear I'm gonna skin you!"

Jett's eyes filled with horror and he broke down.

"All right...He...He's at the Garrett farm."

"You're gonna take us there! Come on, men! Get movin'!"

Most of the men remained crouched in their chairs.

"Get 'em movin', Major!"

Major Doherty and Conger smacked the soldiers to their feet as Baker hurried out with two men holding Jett.

The regiment galloped off.

A silhouette watched the soldiers ride toward the woods. For an instant, the light of the moon revealed his face—the man bore a resemblance to what Booth once looked like with his curly hair and mustache.

He jumped on his horse and galloped wildly toward the Garrett farmhouse as the soldiers approached by another route.

* * *

Lantern in hand, Garrett led Booth and Herold to the barn.

"I'm sorry I've got to put you up in the tobacco shed. I just don't want to bring no trouble on my family."

"We understand, sir. Don't you worry, we'll be gone before sunrise."

Garrett opened the barn door and gave them the lantern.

"It don't get too cold this time of year."

Booth extended his hand.

"Thank you kindly, sir. Goodnight."

"I hope you have a safe journey home," the farmer said with sincerity.

Booth and Herold entered the barn as Garrett returned to the house, worried. His son stood on the front porch.

"Listen, son, I want you to lock those front doors and sleep out near the horses tonight. I don't want to find any of our mares gone with those gentlemen tomorrow."

"Should I block the other doors on the side, Pa?"

"No, just stay near the horses."

Garrett looked back at the barn, troubled, and entered the house.

Booth and Herold sat on the hard floor. Other then a few pieces of furniture stored in a corner, the barn was empty. Booth took off his coat and tried to make himself comfortable.

"You know what they call Mosby's command?"

Herold shook his head.

"The Grey Ghosts," he said with a smile. "It's a good feeling to have them watching over us. Goodnight, Herold."

"Goodnight, Mister Booth."

Herold laid back and folded his arms behind his head. He stared up at the ceiling, confident and relaxed for the first time since their frantic journey began. He closed his eyes peacefully.

Booth leaned against the wall of the barn and wrote a few notes in his diary. He smiled to himself as he thought of the young Confederate lieutenant, John William Boyd, who was stationed nearby ready to come to their aid. Booth was certain that he would soon be safe and the wretched conditions in which they found themselves would be unpleasant memories never thought of again.

He had first met Boyd several years before in one of the secret meetings of the Knights of the Golden Circle south of the Mason-Dixon line. They were initiated into the order on the same night, an event that made them as close as brothers. Booth felt closer to Boyd and his compaions of the secret society than he did to his own blood brothers. He was especially close to John Boyd. They were the same age and even looked alike, except for Boyd's reddish hair. They had both committed their lives to the cause and were willing to give up everything for what they believed to be true justice.

There could have been no better choice than Boyd to make him feel safe in these dangerous moments. He knew that the young man would do anything to help his brother escape the Yankees. They had been on several missions together into Canada, meeting with their English supporters across the border. Together, they had risked their lives smuggling union plans and Confederate money through enemy lines. Booth had witnessed John Boyd's remarkable courage and fearlessness. The man had lost his entire family beneath the sabers of Sherman's troops and threw himself with abandon into the lost cause.

Booth had no doubt that he would come through for him in his hour of need. The leadership of the Knights knew this as well and had honored Booth's request to place his friend at this critical location, the final stage of his escape to the ship that would take him to another continent. Every step was planned and hundreds of people were involved. This was the final act of a people who felt betrayed and destroyed by their own government.

He put his diary back into his jacket pocket and hung it up on the wall of the barn. He checked his watch and waited. David Herold was fast asleep. Booth shook his head at his companion's ability to forget the gravity of their condition and give himself up to sweet dreams. Somehow, he already knew that nature's gift of rest would never be his again, even if everything went according to plan.

He sat there in the darkness listening to the crickets and an owl's haunting cry. For the first time, he felt at peace, so close to the final effort of his escape. It had not been as simple as he had hoped. The pain in his leg refused to go away. But a greater pain was growing in his soul. Fearful doubts howled at the doors of his mind, stimulated by the headlines he had seen. How was it that world had not seen his act for what it was, at least for what he thought it was. Had he not performed a heroic feat and killed a tyrant in the same manner as Brutus had before him? Or had he blackened his name for all time by committing the foulest of deeds? He couldn't bear to deal with these conflicting thoughts. He burned them out with a swig of brandy. He knew that if he thought too long upon these matters, something within him would explode. Why couldn't it be black and white, good and evil, as he had once imagined? He knew few men who would have taken the risks he had and handed over so glorious and prosperous a career for his principles and sense of justice. And yet the country had failed to recognize his sacrifice.

Worst of all were the visions of Ogarita and Izola haunting him like ghosts rising from the grave. How could he have abandoned them along with his career? Was anything worth such devastating sacrifice? Somehow the madness of the war and the fierce loyalties of the secret society had made him drunk with the assumption that these external events were more important than the sweet home he had created.

Now on this dark night, at this decisive moment of his escape, he felt a nauseous vertigo shake his body. Had this self-made nightmare been a terrible mistake? Again he poured the hot liquid down his throat to numb the soul-pain that held him as tight as a hangman's noose. The theater of blood that had gone on for four endless years suddenly seemed as unreal as the plays he had memorized and staged for the public's entertainment. It all seemed so absurd. The wasteful deaths and monstrous destruction, the deep secrets and conspiracies all seemed like some outrageous play written by a fool who had forgotten the true purpose of human existence.

Booth looked up at the high ceiling of the tobacco barn. Soon he would be in a faraway land, surrounded by foreign sounds, scents and faces. This was the opposite result of what he hoped for. He who had loved his country more than life would be doomed to live far from it in lands that were alien and unfriendly. He'd heard the stories of India where British friends had established a foothold for the powerful tea companies. He'd seen the lithographs of strange gods and religions so foreign to his experience. Already in his head he could hear odd music and drumbeats that would remind him with each note of his terrible loss.

Men in turbans appeared to his inner sight. Acrid spices, and dark, ancient alleyways permeated with a sense of hopeless abandonment made his blood run cold. He felt like a child tossed out of his home into a world where nothing was familiar.

He knew that this was a clairvoyant vision of his future. Perhaps it would be better to come out of that barn and face his pursuers with the nobility of the Shakespearean characters he had so often portrayed. Perhaps it would be better to spill his blood on the land that he so dearly loved rather than wander far from it to the end of his days.

He smiled sadly and heard himself laugh at the irony. This elaborate escape seemed to be a worse fate than death itself. What was the point of saving his life in order to suffer these intolerable feelings forever? Such a life was not worth living.

An overpowering sensation struck him as though a bullet had torn through his chest. The words of the ancient curse came back to him: *Behold, Thou has driven me out this day from the face of the earth; and from Thy face shall I be hid; and I shall be a fugitive and a vagabond in the earth.* In that moment, he realized that this would be the justice handed to him for the murder he had committed. Even if he escaped the justice of men, he would never escape the justice of his Maker. Already, he had been branded with the punishment. The Curse of Cain was upon him and he would never be able to escape it. The entire Yankee army was as nothing compared to the doom imposed upon him in response to what he had done.

He forced himself to stand. He looked out through the cracks of the wooden walls. A full moon in a black sky stared down at him like the eye of God, unblinking and all-knowing.

"What have I done?" he said out loud. Sweat suddenly poured down his face, generated from a fire in his soul, a wildfire that would never be extinguished.

He knew that he had to continue on, despite the gloomy future he foresaw. He had chosen his path and he would now have to pay the price, a price that no human court could have brought down upon him. He realized that it could only mean one thing: The man he had killed had been a good man, a righteous man, regardless of their different interpretations of the Constitution and the rights of secession upon which Booth had fanatically placed everything he loved as though playing some reckless poker game.

It was clear to him that he had killed more than a political man, but a man beloved in the spirit realm, a rare man the likes of which so seldom appeared on this earth. Abraham Lincoln was not merely commander-in-chief of the pillaging northern armies, but a God-fearing individual who had also sacrificed himself for the cause he felt was right. Perhaps his cause was greater than Booth's.

Pale moonlight shot into the barn, mercilessly exposing the pale features of the former actor, now a wanted murderer.

"What have I done?" he repeated again.

He thought for a moment that he would pass out under the strain of this encounter with his conscience. He had the urge to grab his pistol and put a hole in his head to end the pain here and now. In an instant, he could wipe out the images of his loved ones that he knew would haunt him always, along with the terrible guilt that already strangled him.

But something within him, even more powerful than his conscience, held him back. Something beyond his will. Something supernatural that would force him to live out the curse to the end of his days.

Booth slumped down into the humid earth, shivering from unspeakable terror. He no longer feared the hordes of Yankees searching for him somewhere beyond the surrounding farmlands. A greater fear had emerged—the sense of a supernatural presence that would require him to live out the consequences of his evil deed to the bitter end. He tried reaching for his pistol, unable to bear the intolerable suffering that tortured his soul. He wanted to defy this strange awareness of a greater power hovering over him, full of judgment and wrath. He wanted to rid himself of the agony he had inflicted on his loved ones, himself, and his country.

His hand trembled so badly that he could barely wrap his fingers around the weapon. He managed to get a good grip on the handle and raised it toward his temple. All of a sudden, he felt a burning sensation in his hand that forced him to release his grip and drop the pistol. He let out a muffled cry of horror.

Trembling uncontrollably, Booth looked over at Herold who kept up his snoring, completely unaware of the traumatic battle in which his companion was engaged. Booth looked back at the gun. Could it be that something was keeping him from acting on his own will? He went for the pistol again and had to pull away as though the gun was on fire.

He looked out through the cracks in the wall and saw the moon watching him. In that moment, he understood that he was not master of his fate. By killing his brother, Abraham, he had placed himself into the hands of a Judge who would never let him go. He had broken a law that would require him to live out every second of just punishment. Booth dropped his head in his hands, wishing that he had taken more seriously the great Shakespeare's spiritual wisdom who had warned men of the omniscient presence of mighty forces in human affairs.

He remembered now his eccentric father's reverence for holy scripture. None of it had penetrated his soul before, blinded as he was by the limelight, the praise of his fellow man, and the vanity of what nature had given him. Now covered with mud and sweat, burning with a spiritual agony that would rage within him forever, John Booth felt the full weight of the justice spoken of from ancient days.

Most people discovered this judgment in the afterlife. But the magnitude of his deed gave him the perverse privilege of tasting it while still alive in the flesh. He had not only killed the President of the United States, but a beloved child of the Creator. Sitting in the shadows of the barn, Booth moaned from the depths of his soul, but it was too late for remorse. All he could do now was live out the consequences.

* * *

A peaceful silence hung over the little farmstead. One of the old horses snorted in the stable. The brilliant moonlight descended upon the rural setting like a gentle blessing from heaven. A faint sound of galloping hooves echoing in the distance broke through the late night quiet.

A shadow suddenly came crashing through the woods, breathing heavily. The man who had been watching the soldiers hurried toward the barn.

A dog barked as the sound of hoofbeats grew louder. They suddenly stopped at a muted command. Shadows rushed up the path to the farm. The dogs now barked ferociously. Boots trampled onto the porch and the metallic jingle of scabbards and spurs destroyed the silence.

The Garrett son, sleeping outdoors near the horses, awoke with a jolt.

Light came on in the house.

"Open up! We've got the house surrounded!" Lieutenant Baker shouted. "We'll shoot our way in."

Garrett appeared at the door in his nightshirt. Baker took hold of him.

"We want those two men! We know they're here!"

"No, they've gone," the farmer responded in a trembling voice.

Baker pinned him against the door. He aimed his revolver in the farmer's face.

"Come up here and get this reb, boys! Maybe a little neck stretching will loosen his tongue!"

The soldiers pushed him into the yard toward a chopping block and forced him onto it. Baker approached the terrified old man.

"We know those assassins are on your place! Where are they hiding?"

"In the woods! In the woods!" the farmer cried out.

"It's your neck! Okay, sergeant, bring the rope."

A soldier fashioned a noose. Garrett noticed Captain Jett, bloody and bound, among the men.

"You done this! You brought them here!"

"Never mind who brought us here! You got one more chance, old fool! Where are the two killers?"

The noose was placed around his neck. The family watching from the porch screamed and begged for mercy. Suddenly, the son rushed out from the shadows.

"I'll take you to them! Don't hurt him!"

He led Baker and his men toward the shed. Conger managed to get a few soldiers to take positions thirty feet from the barn. The others laid on the ground, dead tired. Major Doherty grabbed the boy and ran to the door of the barn.

"Come on out! We know you're in there!" the officer shouted.

"You're surrounded by Federal troops," Baker called out. "You haven't got a chance! We're gonna send the Garrett kid in there and you'll hand over your weapons to him. Walk out after him with your arms lifted. You hear?"

No answer. Baker approached the door and pushed the boy forward. He ordered him to unlock the door. Shaking with fear, the boy obeyed. Baker shoved him through the door and dodged aside to duck any possible gunfire.

After a long wait, the boy finally came out.

"They won't surrender, sir."

The soldiers quickly moved away from the barn.

"All right, men. We want him alive!" Major Doherty ordered.

Baker told the boy to get some brush as Major Doherty barked out instructions.

"Take your position around the side there, Sergeant Corbett. Mr. Conger, if you and Lieutenant Baker take the door, I'll watch the rear. Keep your boys well covered, about ten yards back."

The Garrett boy returned with an armload of brush and followed Conger to the rear of the barn. They cautiously stacked the brush against the wall.

After they returned to the front of the barn, Baker called out again:

"Last chance, you two! Surrender or we'll fire the barn and smoke you out like rats! We'll give you one minute to make up your minds!"

A heavy silence fell over the anxious faces.

The Garrett family watched from the porch. Farmer Garrett was still standing on the chopping block, mortified. The soldiers shifted restlessly.

"Time's up!" yelled Baker. "Come out peaceable or you'll be burned out."

A voice finally came from inside the barn.

"I will never surrender!"

"For God's sake, come out of there!" the Garrett son implored. "You can't escape!"

"Booth, you don't have a chance!" Baker shouted.

The voice spoke again:

"Come on, cowards! All I ask for is a fighting chance!"

"David Herold!" Major Doherty yelled, trying another tactic.

"Come on out! There's no point in this. You're through running."

Whispers were heard in the barn as everyone awaited breathlessly.

"Oh, Captain," the voice called out. "There's a man in here
who wants to surrender awful bad!"

Herold suddenly appeared from the barn, hands raised high
and yelling "don't shoot!"

Major Doherty and a soldier hurried to him and dragged him
off. They tied him to a tree as he shook in terror. Conger carefully
went around the side of the barn and lit the brush. The fire
devoured the dry wood.

"Hey you!" the voice cried out. "I could have shot you when
you came around the barn. But I didn't out of respect because I
know you're a brave officer. Give me fifteen paces and I'll make
good my escape."

The officers were baffled by the man's bravado. The fire rose
up the side of the barn. A shadow could be seen inside. Conger
watched from the side of the barn, pistol in hand. The silhouette
dodged falling pieces of wood, a pistol and rifle in each hand.

Suddenly, the sound of a single shot ripped through the night
air. The shadow fell in a heap. After a moment, Conger peered
through the cracks in the wall. He then rushed in, followed by
Baker and Major Doherty.

They found the man still alive, a bullet in his neck.

"What the hell did you shoot him for?" Baker barked angrily at
Conger.

"I didn't shoot him. He shot himself."

"Are you sure?" Major Doherty asked.

"Well, he was standing there and..."

The three men called out to the soldiers and asked if anyone fired the shot. The men shook their heads. They carried the body out of the barn to the porch. Baker ordered additional light. The Garrett daughter hurried inside to fetch a lantern. Everyone gathered around the wounded man.

The dim light revealed the features of a man with mustache and curly hair, dressed in a confederate uniform.

Baker took out a photograph of Booth.

"That's the man, all right. Where's he been shot?"

Major Doherty lifted his head. Blood soaked the porch.

"In the back of the neck. We may as well get a doctor."

"Who disobeyed orders and shot him?" Baker called out again.

For a moment there was no response. Finally, Sergeant Corbett stepped forward.

"I did," the mongoloid-featured man stated with a strange calm.

"Why did you disobey my orders, sergeant?"

"I was directed by the hand of God," he answered simply.

Conger returned into the barn as the fire died out. He located Booth's overcoat and searched through it. He pulled out the diary from one of the pockets. His eyes grew wide as he leafed through it.

He hurried back to Major Doherty, announcing that he must return to Washington right away.

"What do we do with him?" Baker asked.

Conger kneeled by the wounded man. Garrett's daughter was moistening his lips with a wet handkerchief. The man begged to be put on his side. The daughter and Major Doherty turned him, but he began to gag.

"The other...the other side..."

They turned him again.

"On my face...on my face..."

"We can't put you face down," Conger said coldly.

"I can't stand it! I want to die! Put your hand on my throat."

Conger did so, impatiently. The man tried to cough, attempting to dislodge a splintered bone from his throat. He turned purple, unable to cough.

"Open your mouth," Conger said. "Let me see if you have blood on your tongue."

The man dropped his jaw.

"You haven't been shot through the throat. Your mouth is free of blood."

"Kill me! Kill me!" the wounded man cried out.

"We don't want to kill you," Conger responded cynically. "We want you to get well."

A carriage approached the farm. An old doctor stared out from his carriage, worried by all the grim faces, the smoldering barn, the rope swinging from a tree limb, the filthy soldiers.

He hurried up to the porch and examined the wounded man.

"The bullet punctured his spinal cord."

"How long does he have?" Baker asked. "We don't want to wait all night."

"Not much longer."

The Garrett daughter gently caressed the dying man's forehead.

"Couldn't we give him some water or something?" she wondered sadly.

"I guess, if you want to," Baker stated with disinterest.

"Where are you going to take him?" the doctor asked.

"There's a battleship waiting for us on the Potomac. We'll take him there for positive identification. Then they'll take him back to Washington."

The doctor studied the dying man and looked at the motley group. He shook his head and left. Garrett's son approached his father who had been released and took him aside.

"One of our horses is missing," he whispered.

Garrett could scarcely hold back a look of delight. He managed to control himself and looked back at the porch.

"That's not all," the son continued. "I went looking for the horse and I found this a little ways in the woods."

From under his coat, he produced Booth's field glasses.

"You take 'em in the house, son. And don't you say a word," the old farmer ordered. His son smiled and hurried to the back entrance of the home.

The daughter returned with water and sponged the man's face. She tried to make him drink but the water slid out of his mouth.

Dawn slowly broke across the horizon. Everyone sat near the porch, waiting for the man to die. He gasped for water, but could not swallow what was given to him. Baker paced and chewed his tobacco impatiently. Herold crouched against a tree, whimpering. Finally, as the sun started to rise, the man twitched violently and whispered for the farmer's daughter to hold up his hands before his face. He stared at the lifeless limbs in horror.

"Useless...Useless..." he moaned hoarsely. Then he released a long exhalation and his head fell sideways.

The daughter leaned over him and cut a piece of his thick curls. Tears sparkling in her eyes, she whispered a prayer for the dead man.

Baker motioned for Major Doherty to join him.

"Find us a wagon, Major. I'll take the body and the reb captain through the woods, the quick way. You and the men take the road."

"You don't want an escort, Lieutenant?"

"I'll manage just fine, thank you."

Major Doherty headed out, but suddenly stopped and turned back.

"Say, Lieutenant..."

He approached Baker.

"You'd better do something about that left leg. It's suppose to be broken."

Baker spat and walked back to the porch.

* * *

An old wagon bounced along a dirt path in the woods. The grim dawn had given way to a lovely spring day. Lieutenant Baker was at the reins, guiding the horses through the countryside. Captain Jett sat at his side, hands tied behind his back, his face bruised by the beating.

In the back of the wagon lay the body partly covered by a dirty army blanket. Muddy boots stuck out from under the blanket. Blood soaked into the wood underneath the covered head.

Suddenly, the wagon hit a sharp bump and one wheel broke away. The body slid out the back. Baker cursed, reined in the horses, and jumped from the wagon to fix the wheel. As he repaired it, Jett silently slipped off the wagon, and ran like a wildman for the underbrush. Baker drew his gun.

"Halt! Halt, or I'll shoot!"

Baker shot without aiming, watching Jett disappear. A grin came over his crusty features and he returned to mending the wheel.

He threw the body in the back of the wagon and started off

again. He soon came to the river where a gunboat was docked. Several soldiers approached him as he pulled the wagon to a stop.

"Take that on the deck, corporal," Baker ordered.

The soldiers carried the corpse onto the boat, followed by Baker.

Several officers stood on deck. They quickly surrounded the body. A group of civilians were gathered in a corner, nervous and frightened.

Major Eckert appeared from below and greeted Baker with a warm handshake. One of the officers rolled back the blanket. A photographer came forward to snap a picture of the corpse. Major Eckert shoved him away.

"No pictures! Orders from Washington," he growled.

Dismayed, the photographer moved away under Major Eckert's threatening glare. The Major then leaned over the body. The face was grotesquely distorted by a grimace of pain. Major Eckert looked over at the group of civilians and motioned for them to approach.

"One at a time. Make way, gentlemen."

An agitated man approached the body as the officers cleared the way.

"Is that John Wilkes Booth?"

"I only met him a few times…" the man said with hesitation.

"Is that him?" the burly major barked.

"Well…I think so…"

He didn't dare come too close to the cadaver.

"He won't bite. Take a good look."

The man studied the corpse.

"Are you positive?"

"Yes…"

"Next. Oh, Sergeant, get that man's name."

The man looked back in terror. Another civilian came forward.

"What's your name?"

"Seaton Monroe, sir."

"What relationship did you have with the dead man?"

"I am a lawyer and I met Mister Booth during several transactions."

He examined the body carefully.

"It's difficult to tell. By his general appearance, it could be him."

"Good," Major Eckert said as he moved him away. "Next? Name?"

"Dr. Frederick May. I was his surgeon."

Dr. May stepped over to the body. A surprised look came over his features. He kneeled for a closer look.

"That is not him. That corpse bears no resemblance to him."

The officers crowded in around him with great concern.

"This man's face is freckled," the doctor added.

"Take a good look, doctor," Major Eckert ordered angrily.

"I'm sorry, but..."

"Sir, you were summoned here to identify a scar from a surgical operation you performed on this man. Look at the neck."

Dr. May moved the head to one side. A scar was visible on the neck.

"This scar looks as much like the effects of a burn as it does a cicatrix from an operation."

The agitation among the officers intensified.

"This seems to be the scar of a burn rather than an incision."

"Take another look at the face, doctor," Major Eckert insisted.

"Well, I do recognize the likeness..."

"He recognizes the likeness," Major Eckert victoriously pointed out to the officers.

"But the bullet hole in relation to the scar is…"

"Thank you, doctor. You've helped us immensely."

With that, Dr. May was led away, stammering.

Major Eckert smiled at the other officers. "We now have medical proof, gentlemen. That's good enough for me."

The others approved triumphantly. A breeze fluttered through the corpse's hair, revealing the frozen features of William Boyd, the confederate soldier who had rushed to the Garrett farmhouse ahead of the regiment.

* * *

A man on horseback trotted down the sunbathed path leading to a home situated in peaceful countryside. He stopped by the gate of the house. A figure was on the porch, rehearsing lines for a play. The man watched for a moment, enjoying the performance.

"Hey, Mister Andrews!" he finally called out.

The man on the porch continued his rehearsal, so absorbed in his work that he did not hear him.

"Bill Andrews!"

Andrews turned around, revealing the friendly face of Booth's friend who assisted him on the night of the assassination.

"Hello, Frank! How are you?" Andrews called out, on his way down to the gate to greet him.

"I picked up some mail for you in town this morning. It's been layin' around for a couple of weeks."

"I've been on tour for the past six months, Frank."

The man handed him a small package.

"Oh yeah? How was it?"

Bill Andrews unwrapped it.

"Boston is always a good engagement. But audiences are a little scarce. Our nation's wounds are still healing."

Suddenly, his eyes widened and his lips began to tremble.

"My God, what is it Mister Andrews? Are you all right?" the man questioned, stunned by his reaction. Bill Andrews was paralyzed with shock.

"Are you ill?"

He touched his arm. Andrews did not react. His stupefied attention was glued to the contents of the package. Alarmed, the man peered into the package. He looked back at Andrews, relieved.

"Why, it's only a scarf-pin, Mister Andrews."

Bill Andrews looked up with glazed eyes that did not see him.

"You scared me there for a minute. I thought you'd seen a ghost."

Andrews stared at him vacantly. The man smiled awkwardly under the strange stare.

"Well, I'll be on my way, Mister Andrews. Have a good day."

He backed away, expecting a response. Andrews was no longer aware of his presence. The man shuddered and left quickly.

Bill Andrews looked back down at the package. He took out the cameo scarf-pin from the box and raised it to eye level. It was the very one that he used to wrap Booth's leg the night of the assassination.

He looked out at the horizon, tears running down his cheeks.

SIX

The small seaport on the Island of Ceylon was perched on the edge of a vast expanse of ocean. Despite its distance from the centers of civilization, it was a crossroads for the world's population. The small city teemed with travelers from every continent. Though most of the people were Asian, a variety of foreigners mixed among them—English, French, Australian.

Standing head and shoulders over the milling crowds was the Englishman, William Barrett who had been at Dr. Mudd's house the night that Booth arrived with Herold. He carried a bundle under his arm which had clearly traveled far.

Bartlett stopped in front of a pub reserved for foreigners and strangely out of place in this Asian setting. He pulled out his watch, checked the time, and entered.

The wealthy, continental atmosphere contrasted sharply with the island's poverty. Several men of various European nations sat at tables talking quietly. They wore the clothing of officers, adventurers, and fugitives.

Bartlett sat at a table in one of the darker corners. He took out a cigar, lit it, and waited patiently. The bartender noticed him and disappeared for a moment.

He returned with the establishment's owner, Robert Manchester, a wealthy merchant. The portly owner joined Bartlett at his table and motioned for the bartender to bring them a couple of drinks. They greeted each other warmly.

"Good to see you again, brother. Uneventful trip, I trust?" Manchester asked with a jovial smile.

"I'm getting use to the months at sea now. The only hardship is passing the time."

The bartender served them. They raised their glasses in a toast.

"To our brother and his health," Manchester stated with a sudden melancholy.

"And to the brotherhood that binds us all together," Bartlett whispered.

"Indeed," the merchant agreed as they drank.

"How is our friend these days?"

"I don't have occasion to see much of him. No one does, really. Except his man, Henry. Sad fate for one who lived in front of the footlights, eh?"

"Surely he's happy to be alive, considering the circumstances."

"That's hard to say. Other brothers tell me he's a brooding sort of fellow. Not much for companionship."

"I can understand that. He's left behind everything he cared for."

Bartlett held up the package.

"I'm sure he lives for these letters."

"The worst of it is, his act accomplished nothing. His country might have remembered him for his greatness, but now his name is blackened forever. All for nothing. A man of tragedy, he is."

"What can we do for him?" Bartlett asked with genuine concern.

"Oh, help him to new hiding places when the need is there. But no one can give him his old life back."

Manchester spotted someone through the front windows. A young black man, Henry, stood by the door, anxiety etched on his features.

"There he is," the merchant announced. "You've completed your mission once again, brother."

Bartlett handed him the package.

"Tell him the trip as been arranged."

"Really?" Manchester responded in surprise. "Whom did you find for such a foolish enterprise?"

"There's only one man in the China Sea and Pacific Ocean combined for such an undertaking: Captain William Tolbert."

"Tolbert? Bill Tolbert who defeated the Yankees with his Shenandoah battleship?"

"Precisely," Bartlett stated with confidence. "I'd call him more of a gentleman pirate than a war hero, though."

"I must say, with Captain Tolbert at the helm, this madness just might succeed."

He looked over at Henry who stood on the sidewalk, awkward and nervous.

"We best not keep that poor young man waiting. His nerves will get the best of him," the merchant whispered.

They stood and shook hands.

"Will you accompany him on this trip?" Manchester asked.

"I'm afraid not. Too much danger for my blood. Between you and me, this is the last wish of a dead man."

"Indeed. A living dead man. That's what our poor brother has come to. He would have done better to die in a battlefield for his beloved South."

The merchant shook his head sadly and went to the front door. He stepped out and greeted Henry coolly, handing him the package.

"Tell your master that his journey is set."

Henry's face brightened. He could hardly contain his exhilaration.

"I'm not so sure I've given you good news, Henry. There is no guarantee of safety this time."

"I understand, sir. But it's home...it's home!"

"There is no home for your master," Manchester said somberly. "You best be going. Tell him I wish him well."

He pulled out another package from his pocket.

"Give him this token of my friendship. I can do no more for him. Others will be watching over him now."

"Thank you, sir," Henry said with warm gratitude sparkling in his tired eyes. "Thank you for all you've done."

Henry left quickly, looking back for a final glance. The merchant watched him disappear in the crowd. He shook his head sadly and returned into the pub.

* * *

The opium den was dimly lit by many candles, but even that light was veiled by the cloud of toxic smoke roaming through the room. Wretched men lay on the floor next to strange urns filled with the poison that helped them escape their reality. They were from different races and lands but all had in common haunted, gaunt faces and vacant eyes. Unclean prostitutes sat at the side of some of the addicts.

There were several Americans in the dank room. One of them was sitting at a bar in the far end of the room, puffing on a cigar and sipping liquor. Another moved slowly through the room, attempting to converse with the human waste that made up the den's clientele. He was a missionary seeking to find a lost lamb he could remove from this deadly abyss.

The man at the bar spotted a third American among the faces of addicts puffing away. The man had long, curly hair and a black beard. The wild curls couldn't hide the features of John Wilkes Booth. Prematurely aged, his dark eyes were permanently overcast with a deep, unsettling look of melancholy. He was the classic portrait of a fugitive, a wanderer without home or family. His intensity was all the more acute due to an agonizing remorse over his mad act that killed a great man and ruined a promising life.

"I'll bet you're a runaway reb, ain't you?" the burly man at the bar said in a mocking voice. "I seen a dozen of your leaders in these parts. Y'all got what you deserve!"

Booth turned his hazy gaze upon the drunken troublemaker. Fire returned to his bloodshot eyes.

"I was with Sherman in Atlanta," the man continued as he stepped away from the bar. "I saw it all burn to the ground! I'll never forget how good it felt. I helped set it with my own hands!"

Before he completed his sentence, Booth was on his feet. The drug-induced blurriness in his eyes had vanished completely. Outrage burned in its place. The large man bit down on his cigar, his jaw muscles flexing with eagerness for a fight. He clenched his fists, ready to strike. But he hadn't counted on his adversary's fury.

A silver blade flashed in the dim candlelight. The knife came out of nowhere and sliced open the man's right cheek. He let out a shout and grabbed his face. Booth's knuckles slammed against his temple and the man fell to his knees, helpless as a puppet cut from its strings. A woman screamed and addicts scrambled away from the dark stranger with the eyes of fire.

Only the missionary stood nearby, tense with fear, but entranced by the sight of the soul, wild with pain and rage, before him.

Booth spat on his fallen adversary and looked over at the clergyman who flinched beneath his smoldering glare.

"I won't hurt you!" Booth projected with the melodrama that still remained in his mannerisms despite the death of his life as a classical actor.

"Do you believe in God?" the missionary blurted out, more out of concern for his life than for the sake of Booth's soul.

"I've become a believer..." Booth mumbled cynically.

"You have?" the man responded with surprise, looking him over from head to foot and seeing nothing but a wretched vagabond full of liquor and dissipation.

"I believe wrong is punished," Booth said with tragic resignation, moving toward the clergyman and disregarding the man who had so roused his anger.

"That is self-evident," the missionary responded, nodding accusingly to the bleeding man on the floor.

"I don't mean punished by human beings."

"You mean in some kind of afterlife?"

"I mean here and now."

"Well, there's the hangman's rope..."

"I told you I wasn't talking about human justice! I mean divine judgment!"

"Are you a Bible reader, friend?"

"Do I look like that to you?" Booth responded, shooting at him a look that could kill.

"So what do you know about that subject, then?"

"More than you'll ever want to know, I can assure you."

"I'm a preacher, a missionary of the Word! How dare you tell me a thing like that!"

Booth stepped up to him, nearly touching the man's face with his.

"Reverend," he said, exhaling an odor of stale liquor that could melt paint from a wall, "I know there's a Hell because I'm living in it. And there's nothing you or anybody else can do about it."

"There's always redemption, son," the missionary replied, disturbed by the desperation he saw in Booth's bloodshot eyes.

"Not for me, there isn't. I have to pay the price."

The missionary placed his hand on Booth's shoulder. "I've known men who have done terrible things, but they've always been given a second chance. That's the gospel I know."

"I've had my chance, and I lost it all!"

The missionary moved his hand away, shocked by the man's inner turmoil. Booth smiled sadly.

"Don't worry, preacher. I don't think it's contagious."

The clergyman couldn't think of anything to say to him.

"You don't want to know the likes of me, Mister Preacherman. It would put you out of business. There are souls that the Almighty will not look upon anymore."

"That's not what it says in my Bible," the missionary said with as much conviction as he could muster.

"Then just look at my Bible!" Booth cried out. He tore open his shirt, revealing a chest mangled with deep scars. "Do you know what this is, reverend? These are tracks made by my own fingers trying to tear my heart out. That one right there was written with a Turkish knife, the sharpest in the world. But I can't do it, not because I don't want to, but because I'm not allowed!"

Booth pointed upwards, eyes glazed with agony. "He's making me live!"

The missionary turned a pale grey and his lower lip trembled. He took two steps backwards.

"He wants me to live and endure His curse! There's no church that's going to help me out of that!"

The missionary was about to turn away, but he had to try one more time. He held up his ragged black leather Bible.

"This is a book of forgiveness and redemption! I've seen it work!"

Booth approached him. "It may have worked on natives who didn't know any different. How many of them put a derringer bullet in the back of a man's head from three feet away?"

"What kind of a beast are you?" the missionary cried out, stepping back in horror.

"The worse kind! Abandoned by God Himself!"

The missionary hurried off through the crowded street, pushing people out of his way to get as far as possible from this man of darkness.

Booth snickered and stumbled out of the den, heading for the thick foliage where he could hide his shame.

* * *

Henry hurried through the jungle-like vegetation that surrounded the seaport and made his way to a small home buried in the thick brush. He let out a special whistle as he approached. Booth awaited him in the cottage.

Henry entered the hut and handed him the package. Booth tore it open feverishly.

"They'll help us make the trip, Mr. Booth."

"I knew they wouldn't refuse me."

With trembling hands, Booth opened the letters from America. Henry watched him sadly as tears filled the desperate man's eyes.

"My beloved Izola...And my sweet Ogarita. She's nine years old now, Henry."

"She must be a lovely child."

"Listen to what my darling writes:

`I have another life I long to meet,

Without which Life my life is incomplete.

Oh, sweeter self, like me art thou astray,

Trying with all thy heart to find the way,

To mine; straying, like mine, to find the breast

On which alone can weary heart find rest.'"

Booth wept as he kissed the letter.

"We may see them soon, Mr. Booth," Henry whispered gently.

"God willing, Henry, God willing. But it may make the pain of separation worse. Maybe it's better if they forget me. If little Rita forgets what her father looks like."

"Don't say that, Mr. Booth! Think of what those letters tell you. And besides, I'd give anything to see my mammy again. Just once."

Booth grabbed his friend's arms passionately.

"If we make it home, I want you to stay with them, Henry."

"No, Mister Booth, I couldn't leave you!"

"There's no reason for you to be condemned to this terrible wandering. You shouldn't suffer my punishment anymore."

"I've been with you since childhood, and I'll stay with you until one of us is dead."

"No, Henry. I would be happier if I knew you were with my family. It would make me feel closer to them. When we met in

London after my escape, I thought the brotherhood would take us to one port of call and we'd start to live again. But I've dragged you through Calcutta, Shanghai, across the Pacific and Indian Oceans. Enough is enough. I want you to go home and stay home."

"I couldn't bear it! I couldn't think of you alone, with no one..."

"I've got the brotherhood. Their influence extends across most of East Asia. I'll be taken care of."

"I won't do it, Mr. Booth!

"You will, Henry. Now let's see what the plans are."

He pulled out an envelope from the package and read through the materials that include a map.

"We leave in three days on the "Ocean Bird." We dock in San Francisco for just a few hours. And then on to Mexico. My final destination is Bombay."

He looked up at Henry tearfully.

"A few hours..."

"I'll pack your things, Mister Booth," Henry said as he hurried to the bamboo closet.

Booth staggered out into the light and wandered in the exotic foliage.

The statue of a god of war stood by the moss-covered temple. Booth approached the statue and studied its features. They were full of violence and hate. He touched the sword.

A priest in yellow robes appeared from behind the statue as though out of nowhere, and looked piercingly at Booth.

"You know my thoughts, old man," Booth said after a moment.

"I have never seen such darkness in a man's soul before."

"I'm a victim of this god. I've been a servant to his violence."

"There is great karma to be worked upon for you."

"Yes...But not in other lives as you believe. I have sinned in this life and in this life I pay the price."

"If you feel such remorse, my son, why do you still worship death?"

"I seek peace..."

"You will not find it in death. You will only find recurrence. Peace must be found now, in this moment."

"If the Curse of Cain follows me beyond death, then I am truly doomed."

"The Curse of Cain?"

"From the Christian Scriptures..."

He looked away with great melancholy.

"Behold, Thou has driven me out this day from the face of the earth; and from Thy face shall I be hid; and I shall be a fugitive and a vagabond in the earth."

The priest's eyes darkened, sensing the evil act that weighed so heavily upon Booth's soul. He whispered a prayer in his language and hurried off. He looked back at Booth who remained in a trance-like state. The priest whispered another prayer and rushed away.

Booth studied the statue and its evil expression of hatred and violence.

"God forgive me...God forgive me..." he muttered tearfully.

* * *

Ornate candlesticks rocked back and forth as the ship was tossed by powerful waves. Thunder and heavy rain beat down on the deck above the captain's quarters.

The paraphernalia of a buccaneer sea captain's quarters

crammed the small room with treasures from across the world. Captain William Tolbert was a middle-aged man radiant with robust energy and devil-may-care bravado. His face was permanently marked by windburn and scars of vicious battles. He took a swig of whiskey and stared at his brooding guest.

"I'm told that you rode with the Richmond Greys. Did you see any action?"

Booth sat across the table from him. He had shaved his beard and cut his hair so that he looked like the Booth of old, except that his handsome features were fading beneath the weight of the pain in his soul which he bore constantly. He wore the dark, elegant clothing that distinguished him in theater circles and he studied the captain as he drank heavily.

"I carried messages across Union lines for Mister Thompson, Secretary of War of the Confederacy."

"But did you see any action?"

"I was at Harper's Ferry and assisted in the capture of John Brown."

He took another drink, as though washing down the burning memories.

"I led two kidnap attempts on Lincoln, hoping to exchange him for Confederate prisoners. But we failed and were left with no alternatives."

"So you sent the Yankee tyrant straight to Hell!"

Booth took a big swig.

"I'm not sure who was sent to Hell."

"What's that you say? Speak up. The canons have affected my hearing."

"Lincoln was the lucky one."

Captain Tolbert exploded with coarse laughter.

"The lucky one! That's a good one! Don't feel so sorry for yourself, Mister Booth. Your life ain't so bad. You'll like Bombay. Just stay out of the sun and don't touch the water."

He drank and held up the bottle.

"Keep plenty of this around."

Booth glared at him. Captain Tolbert leaned over the table toward him.

"Wanderin' the seas is my life. I don't understand the need for a piece of ground to call home. And who needs a wife to tie you down, eh? I know a man like you can find women whenever he wants one. Besides, those gentlemen of the Freemasonry, or whatever the hell their secret club is, they own half the bordellos from here to China."

"You have no idea what you're saying, Captain Tolbert. Surely you know better than to speak on this subject."

"You think I'm frightened by those aristocrats and their religious mumbo jumbo?" the sea captain cried out, suddenly angered. "When they want their dirty work done, who do you think they call on? Not on their fancy "brothers"! No sir! They call on lowly born Bill Tolbert."

"Am I the dirty work you're referring to?" Booth asked coldly.

"With all due...respect, I usually don't travel with murderers as my cargo."

Booth jumped up, enraged.

"I've had enough of your base talk!"

"What'd I say? Ain't that what you are?"

"I'm a son of the Confederacy, as you were before you started trading in whores and opium!"

"Don't you judge me! I shot my enemies face to face, not in the back!"

Booth raised his arm to strike him.

"You wanna see your family, Booth?" Tolbert asked as he stared intently at his assailant.

Booth hesitated.

"Then sit down and behave yourself!"

Booth barely managed to control his anger and dropped into his chair.

"Come now, we were just having a friendly talk. I'm a blunt sort of man. I don't have no profound, mysterious conversations like your high and mighty friends. I say it plainly."

Booth took a big swig of whiskey.

"And I'll have you know that the cargo that you have such disdain for is paid for mostly by your brothers."

"Nonsense. My friends are men of honor and high ideals."

"You think because they helped the South and smuggled its leaders out that they're clean and proper? I don't know what you do in your secret meetings, but I'm tellin' you, your "brothers" are businessmen and they know where the money is."

"The Knights of the Golden Circle are not traders in narcotics and women! Our organization is as old as the pyramids. Our members are enlightened individuals who are versed in the knowledge of the great…"

"They ain't that enlightened. What good did it do to kill Lincoln? Turns out he would have been the South's best friend after the war! You all left us at the mercy of the carpetbaggers and the anti-reconstructionists. In fact, I wouldn't be surprised if you played right into their hands!"

Booth was aghast at the thought.

"The South fought nobly and was defeated. After you killed Lincoln, it was raped and humiliated. I didn't care much for that

Yankee leader, but he had a good heart, and when it stopped beating, that's when the suffering really started."

Booth's lips trembled in horror at the results of his act. The sound of thunder crashed ominously overhead.

"So why'd you do it? You had everything. Why'd you throw it all away on a lost cause?"

Booth stared at him silently, feeling his throat tighten. He did his best not to show his emotions. The salty old pirate felt sorry for the gentleman vagabond who had nothing left to live for.

"Have you ever been to Richmond in the spring?" Booth asked as his eyes turned dreamy and images of a vanished world floated through his mind. "Or have you seen the belles of Atlanta parading down the street with their silk parasols?"

The man smiled, recalling his own pictures of the South in its glory days.

"This was a gentile civilization. Nothing like the cold, grey North and its industries turning the skies black with their smoke. There was gracefulness among the people and in the very architecture of their homes. Time seemed to slow down there, until the Yankees marched in with their bloody sabers and bayonets."

"That culture was built on the backs of slaves," Tolbert responded, revealing an unexpected trait of humanity beneath his harsh appearance.

"The real issue had to do with the Constitution of the United States. The Federal government claimed a power it had no right to wield. I saw them destroy an entire world that will never be seen again. The South was always my favorite place to stage my plays. The audiences were different. Some of the happiest moments in my life were those starlit nights, strolling down the streets of any southern city. Boston or Philadelphia were too busy with none of the civilities of the southern ways they crushed under their boots. I couldn't bear the loss of that beautiful world. It will never return. Nothing was worth such destruction. The slavery issue could have been dealt with differently."

"Slavery kept that southern culture running smoothly for your romantic walks."

Booth looked into the weather-beaten face of the aging pirate. A shock wave went through him as he realized that the brigand before him was more humane than he was.

"What made you an abolitionist?" Booth finally asked.

"I captained some of those slave ships years ago coming off the west coast of Africa to the seaports of the South. I saw what was done and how those people were treated. I've never seen anything worse in my life. It still gives me nightmares. I don't claim to be anything but a sinner, but I know the Almighty would never forgive such treatment of other human beings. If your Confederate friends wanted their cotton picked, they should have done it themselves, instead of turning to that evil practice."

Booth felt a new level of shame crush his innards. It wasn't enough that he had ruined his own life by shooting a man in the back like a coward, but now he had to face the obscenity of his misguided views as well.

"You would have been an abolitionist too, Mr. Booth, if you'd seen what we had to do to them children who were torn away from their families and their homeland. They were always sick with some disease or other. I felt more sorry for those who didn't die on the voyage than for those who did. They did things to those people that no one would do to animals. And I looked into their eyes too many times to think that they weren't just like us. No sir, that practice had to end, whatever it took."

Booth had never seen a slave auction, and had never realized the degree of human misery hidden below the fine lifestyles of plantation owners he had known. Captain Tolbert enjoyed watching his guest turn sick with guilt at the wretchedness of the cause he had fought for. For the first time in his life, the old sailor felt himself morally superior to a "gentleman" who had always despised his kind. He bared his brown teeth in a mocking smile, feeling as though he had placed a final stake in the proud heart of the once adulated actor.

SEVEN

Near the city of San Francisco, a desolate cliff overlooked the Pacific Ocean beneath black skies torn open by a pale full moon. A carriage made its way up one of the steep hills. A young girl looked out the window with great anticipation.

The other passengers in the carriage included Sarah, the black governess and mother of Henry; Booth's elderly mother; and a strong-willed woman with beautiful, Spanish eyes—Izola, Booth's wife.

"I don't know how much longer I can stand this ride," Mrs. Booth complained. "My back is in terrible pain."

"We're almost there, Mrs. Booth. Look, there's the ocean," Sarah said with affection.

"Can you see my Daddy?" the little girl asked excitedly.

"Not yet, darlin'. But we'll see him soon," Izola told her daughter softly.

She looked out at the magnificent sunset over the vastness of the sea. The carriage came to a halt at the top of a barren cliff rising over the Pacific Ocean. The driver jumped out and checked his watch. He looked toward a small path coming up from one of the many hidden beaches on the coast. The driver pulled out a whistle and sounded a special signal.

Two silhouettes appeared from the shadows and hurried up

the path. The driver opened the carriage door.

"They're here," he called out.

The women descended from the carriage. Little Ogarita ran toward the cliff to look out at the ocean.

"Is my Daddy here?"

The driver smiled sadly and pointed toward the path. The women let out cries of joy as they saw Booth and Henry, drenched and muddy, heading toward them.

Booth released a terrible moan of despair upon seeing his wife and daughter. He ran toward them. Little Ogarita was the first to reach him, and she jumped into his arms.

"Daddy! Daddy! Why did you leave me?"

"Oh, my sweetheart...My little sweetheart," Booth whispered as he wept.

Izola hurried to them and stopped a few feet away. Her strong will wavered as she tried to control herself. Booth turned to her and they exchanged a powerful look of love and agony.

He approached her and touched her face without a word. Izola raised a trembling hand and removed a curl from his eyes. Her trembling fingers moved across his face, tracing the shape she knew so well. Overwhelmed, she suddenly shrieked in despair and crumbled. Booth took hold of her and tried to comfort her.

"My beloved! My life!"

All three wept together in a tight embrace. Booth's mother stood in the shadows, watching. A tear silently slid down her cheek.

"Mother!" Booth called out as he noticed her. He reached out to her, unable to move past the force of his loved ones' embrace. His mother refused to approach him as her pain turned to bitterness.

"Why? Why did you have to destroy us all?"

Booth looked at her in hopeless despair. He knew her condemnation was just. He slowly came near to her, dragging along his wife and daughter.

"Forgive me, Mother..."

Her unspeakable agony suddenly erupted and she struck him across the face.

"How could you do this to us? How could you soil our name and our lives forever?"

"Mary..." Izola whispered tenderly, trying to calm her.

"God damn you for what you've done!" the old woman shouted at her son.

"He has, Mother, He has."

Little Ogarita looked up from her father's shoulder and stopped crying at the sight of her grandmother's pain.

"It's all right, Grandmama. We're all together now. We can be a happy family again."

Her father caressed her hair and kissed her on the forehead.

"No, sweet Rita...I cannot stay."

Ogarita vehemently wrapped her arms around his neck.

"You have to! You have to!"

"Where will they take you?" Izola asked, solemnly facing their fate.

"Bombay..."

"Let us come with you."

"Oh, yes, Daddy! Please let us go with you to Baybay," little Ogarita insisted.

"My fate is dreadful enough as it is. I can't make others endure it too. I should have stayed at the Garrett farm and let them kill me!"

"Don't say that, Daddy!" his daughter cried out.

"Johnny," Mrs. Booth intoned, "you were the light of my heart. But I'd rather know that you were in that grave they say you're in than know that you're banished from us, wandering in foreign lands. There's no end to the pain now. Why did you have to do such a terrible thing?" she asked as she broke down.

"I thought it would help...I thought it would avenge all the wrongs."

"You could have been the greatest actor in the land," his mother told him, "greater even than your father!"

"There could be no glory on the stage for me, Mother. Not when the real world lies bleeding at our feet. When I saw brother killing brother, and fields covered with the bodies of young men barely out of childhood, I knew I could never again put up with the fantasy of the theater. My God, a whole culture was trampled into ashes right before our very eyes!"

"Your brother Edwin is playing Hamlet to packed houses all across the country now. His tour through Europe was a sublime success. He has taken your place as the greatest talent of his generation."

"Let him have it. I chose to follow my conscience!"

"So you murdered a great man! A man our country needed as much as it needed George Washington!"

Mrs. Booth's legs gave way as she fainted and fell in the mud. Henry and the driver gently lifted her up and carried her to the carriage. Her faithful maid Sarah tried to revive her with smelling salts.

"What's the matter with Grandmama?" asked little Ogarita, confused and shaken.

"She's very sad, darling, as we all are," her mother answered in a tired voice.

"See," the girl said, turning to her father, "you can't leave us. Or we'll never be happy again."

"I want you to remember that your Daddy will love you every day, forever, no matter where he is. You and your mother will be my only thoughts."

"But I won't be able to hug you!"

Booth picked her up in his arms.

"I love you so much! Someday maybe you'll understand."

He took Izola's trembling hand.

"Have they taken care of you?"

"Yes," Izola answered coldly. "John Stevenson has given me his name for security and for Ogarita's future."

"I knew we could count on John. Let him know my deepest gratitude."

"It doesn't ease the pain, John. Why can't we go with you? Nothing could be worse than what we're living now."

"There's nothing left in the world for me except the two of you. But to make you cross the seas and move from place to place in lands where even the barest necessities for civilized existence are unknown...That I cannot do."

He took her in his arms and kissed her for a long while.

"I'm a ghost, Izola, a ghost still bearing his carcass with him. Shakespeare himself never dreamt of such a sorry sight. And in my misery, the only glimmer of beauty is the thought of my beloved. To see you in hiding and among loathsome people who trade in fugitives would be too much to bear."

"I would follow you into Hell itself!"

"With Ogarita at your side? No, you mustn't. When Captain Boyd came to the Garrett farmhouse and died in my place...as I made my way to the ship awaiting me, I swore that I would never again let anyone bear my fate. I can't tell you how many times I have awakened from my nightmares with the face of my valiant friend in my mind's eye, holding off the Yankees until he knew I was safe. And then giving up his life. I didn't deserve such sacrifice."

He placed his head on Izola's chest and wept.

"When we met during the war," she murmured, trying to fight off the pain, "I knew that no matter how much you loved me, the South came first. Your passion for the cause was part of what I loved in you."

Booth violently lifted up his head and looked deeply into her eyes.

"But you didn't know that I would be called a madman and a murderer, and be damned for all time! Or that you would have to live with a secret as black and burdensome as any woman ever carried!"

Izola tried to comfort him as he shook with remorse.

"I knew that the war, the theater, other women would come between us. But what binds us together is not broken by the events of this world. It comes from beyond this life, even from beyond death."

She kissed him and looked deeply into his eyes.

"Our souls were bound together from the first day of Creation. Your friends talk of other lives to be lived. From the moment I saw you, I knew you. I knew you as though we had lived and loved and died before. I knew you as a part of me. And my love for you came back to me like a forgotten dream, like all the hopes of my youth blossoming at once."

Booth hugged her.

"Beloved Izola…"

"And somehow I also knew that such a love would bring great pain with it. I saw that giving myself to you would be a marvelous blessing and an awful sacrifice. And I chose to walk that path. I chose this misery so that I could live such love with you for a little while."

"You are too good for the likes of me."

"Our love is my purpose for being. Had I avoided it for the sake of peace and comfort, I would have despaired more than I do now."

"I never meant to hurt you so," Booth managed to mutter between sobs. "I thought that after the war we would settle in a peaceful valley somewhere and grow old together. Nothing was worth throwing this all away. Nothing! And worse still, nothing was accomplished by this mad act."

Izola took his head in her hands and turned it toward their daughter.

"This little girl will only know love for her Daddy. All the rest will be secondary. Whatever history says of you, whatever the Almighty does to you, nothing will stop her from loving you."

"Someday I hope you will forgive me for what I've done to you and to our country."

"I forgive you, Daddy," Ogarita said innocently. "I just want to be with you."

"Hold me!" Booth cried out, "hold me tight!"

They hugged each other desperately. A cold ocean breeze rushed around them as they huddled together in the warmth of their love.

Sarah and Henry assisted Mrs. Booth into the carriage. The driver looked on sadly as he readied his horses for departure. The sea wind flapped through Booth's cape as he hugged his loved ones for the last time.

Booth stumbled down the path to the rocky shore where a rowboat awaited to take him back to the ship anchored nearby. It seemed to him that he'd left a part of himself on that windswept plateau. His body felt empty, just a mass of nervous sensations dominated by a crushing despair that would never leave him.

Little Ogarita called out above the crash of waves over the shores below.

"Don't leave me, Daddy! Don't leave me!"

His little girl's cries would ring in his ears for the next thirty years — unrelenting and as wrenching as they were on this dreadful night. He thought he had suffered these last few years for his crime. But the worse was yet to come. And all he could do was walk into the torture without looking back.

Booth realized in that moment that a living death awaited him and he was eager to taste the horrific punishment.

The lonely silhouette got into the rowboat and glided through the black, choppy waters that reflected the future awaiting him.

EIGHT

A wretched vagabond scurried through the misty cobblestone streets of London. His clothing bore the marks of long travel and nearly subhuman disregard for personal grooming. He slithered through the shadows of the city and made his way to a wealthy neighborhood lined with mansions. This specter of poverty and disrepute made a shocking contrast to the clean and luxurious surroundings.

He knocked at the door with a trembling hand.

William Bartlett answered. His jaw dropped open.

"What are you doing here? How did you find me?"

"Never mind that. Why haven't you responded to my letters?"

"You know what the arrangement was. There was to be no communication, except through intermediaries."

"I want to talk to the leaders of the brotherhood."

"They don't want to have anything to do with you anymore."

"Why not? What happened to the oath of brotherhood?"

"John, they consider you a dead man. You don't exist."

"What are you talking about? I'm standing right in front of you! I'm flesh and blood!"

"According to the history books, there is no more John Wilkes Booth. He's dead and buried. You have no identity and therefore you're not on the rolls of the brotherhood anymore."

Booth slammed his fist against the wall. "How can they do this to me after what I did for them? I gave everything to the cause!"

"You volunteered. No one forced you."

"But I accomplished the mission set out for me. Isn't that worth something?"

"Why would the brotherhood want you back?" the Englishman said haughtily. "Look at yourself. You're a wretch. There's nothing left of who you once were."

Booth straightened himself up and his battered, exhausted face took on an air of royal dignity.

"I am still John Wilkes Booth, son of Junius Brutus Booth, the finest actor of my generation."

"John Wilkes Booth is dead, get that through your skull! You're a sewer rat, a beggar. We don't want your kind in the brotherhood. How do you think you would fit in with members of Parliament and of the Royal family? The brotherhood has no room for the likes of you."

"You cannot abandon me too!" Booth cried hoarsely.

"We've given you money and safe passage. There's nothing more we can do for you. If you insist on coming back to the continent, you're completely on your own."

"I could expose you and your secret conspiracies!"

"Do you think anyone is interested in those old war stories now?" Bartlett answered mockingly. "The Civil War is long over. People are not interested in revisiting the past. Our brotherhood has changed as well. And so have you for that matter, Mister Booth."

"All I want is my due," Booth muttered, "and you'll never see me again."

"What do you think you're owed?"

"Some respect!"

"For shooting a man with his back to you?"

Booth tore his own hair out with fury. "That's not what you called it when we agreed to the plan!"

"Like I said, this is ancient history. A new century is upon us. Besides, we did hold up our end of the bargain. We took care of your loved ones."

"I gave you my youth, my career, my family…"

"Perhaps we all got carried away with the insanity of the times."

"Where do I go now?" Booth asked with a desperate, lost look in his eyes.

"Go back to India. We'll get you onto the next ship. Believe me, that would be best for all concerned. No one wants you here."

"I want to go back to my country!" Booth said as tears rolled down his cheeks.

"Don't be foolish."

"What about when I'm old? Nobody will know."

"Why go back? You won't find anyone alive that you once knew."

"At least I'll be home."

"There is no home on this earth for you, don't you understand that? Go back to Bombay and you'll receive your allotment as before. If it's not enough, we'll increase it."

"I don't want your damn money!" Booth shouted with animal rage. "You used me and betrayed me! You'll be judged as well some day!"

Bartlett shrugged. Booth suddenly felt overcome with shame at his situation. He couldn't tolerate seeing himself turn into a whimpering beggar. He spat at the wealthy English gentleman and rushed away from his home.

Blind with rage and despair, he crossed into the street without looking. A carriage nearly struck him. The driver pulled on the reins with all his might.

"What are doing, fool! You'll get yourself killed!"

Booth looked up about to cry out that this was exactly his aim. One of the passengers peered out the window. It was his brother Edwin. John froze as he caught sight of the familiar face. Edwin's eyes enlarged with shock and he turned deathly pale. For a moment that seemed like eternity, the two brothers stared at each other. John was a tragic sight—unshaven, unclean, dark circles under his eyes, and in filthy rags. Edwin was the very image of success and dignity. His brother's pain went through him like a spear. Tears sparkled in his eyes and fell like a mighty waterfall.

Edwin threw something in the street and shouted for the driver to hurry on. The carriage bounced past John Booth and spattered mud all the way up his legs. He caught a glimpse in the window of several other members of his family. But his brother's face had turned to stone. John looked back in the street where a thick roll of bills lay on the cobblestone. For an instant, he thought of kicking it into the sewer. Then he picked it up and knew that he would guzzle it down to the last farthing as quickly as possible.

* * *

He knew he couldn't last much longer. His heart had been constricted with the agony of his deed and of his condemnation. For so long now, his chest was a permanent knot. It didn't take a doctor to know that it would eventually implode on itself. The liquor he poured through his system had surely burnt holes in his stomach and liver. He was shocked that he was still alive and was certain that this phenomenon was also a part of the curse that had fallen upon him for his evil deed.

John Booth aged quickly. At thirty-five, he looked fifty. And by the time he had limped his way to fifty, he would look seventy. Every day was a gruesome, gnawing torture, body and soul. His heart ached for the touch of loved ones, and his body was filled with the toxic mixture of alcohol and despair. The aquiline features of his former beauty still remained like scarred ruins. The rest of his face was marred with deep wrinkles and dark circles that reflected the black abyss of his soul. The man had lost everything. He was a living corpse who somehow couldn't die.

Why wouldn't he end it as his friends expected him to? Because some recess of his spirit wanted him to suffer and pay each minute of every day for his crime. He had become his own torturer.

The man's unhappy state made even the tramps and vagrants in the back alleys where he wandered turn and gaze at this lost and damned soul. The prostitutes that he sometimes mingled with found his darkness unbearable. Though he was more handsome than most of their clients, they would have nothing to do with him after the first time. The blackness in his soul was too shattering, even for them.

He'd been in numerous drunken brawls over the years. In every sink hole he wandered through, he gained a reputation as an especially dangerous man. Rumors circulated that he actually enjoyed pain and carried a deathwish that made him fearless. The results were usually catastrophic for his assailants.

All that was left of the gentlemanly manners of his youth were a taste for fine clothing and an aristocratic way of eating his food. But the clothes were always tattered and the food always sparse. Most of the time, he was red-eyed, unshaven and fuming with self-loathing.

The worst ruffians of east London stayed away from him. He was a man with no name, no past, no future. In Shanghai, they called him "Mad Dog." In Paris, he inspired a man to write a story about a phantom in the bowels of a theater.

Then one day he vanished altogether, even from the catacombs of society. By that time no one from his past had any more contact with him, and no person on earth knew that he was alive. No one cared. His last wish was to end his cursed existence in the land of his birth.

EPILOGUE

1903 — Somewhere in the Southwest

I came across him somewhere in the Texas plains. He owned a small saloon in a godforsaken town whose name escapes me. The year was 1903 and I was at that age when wanderlust fills the soul with a hunger for adventure and new horizons. As my father was a wealthy industrialist back East, I had the financial resources to explore the lesser known parts of the country. So at age twenty-five, I set out to discover the North American continent which had, only thirty-four years before, embroiled itself in a bloody nightmare known in the history books as the Civil War.

I headed west since the saying "go west young man" had not yet outlived its meaning. My journey took me through the peaceful cornfields of the Midwest and the wheat oceans of Kansas and Oklahoma. Three months of travel soon wore me out and the lack of real adventure and excitement was beginning to dry up my fantasies of what I would find. But then it suddenly happened. As I crossed over into Texas, a strange feeling came over me, like a flash of clairvoyance which I took at first to be the result of heat stroke. Whatever it was, I knew that if I kept heading through the desolate prairies I would discover some great mystery. What I didn't realize was that the mystery would be in the shape of a man, an old man who carried a dark and terrible burden.

When I finally reached the town, I headed straight for the hotel in great need of a bath and a soft bed. But as I past the saloon, my attention was drawn by the echo of a voice, a magnificent voice reciting Shakespeare like no one I had ever heard. My father had taken me many times to the theater in New York where the very best actors of the day had thrilled us with their portrayal of the bard's immortal characters. Yet here, in this lost, sunbaked no man's land, I was overhearing Macbeth's soliloquy with a passion and flair that I had never heard before on any stage.

I quickly limped into the saloon, and as I was covered from head to foot with dust and sweat, I fit right in with the crowd. For a moment, I found myself completely blind. I stood in the dark saloon surrounded by this voice which made my spine tingle with chills. I noticed my heartbeat increase with the troubling feeling that I was in some kind of deeply unsettling dream, the kind which, on waking, leaves you with the feeling of being hopelessly lost and confused. As my eyes adjusted to the low light streaming in from small, dingy windows, I noticed a dozen cowboys sitting at tables playing cards and gulping hard liquor.

In the far corner there were several fearsome men, some of them in Mexican clothing, all of them unshaven, scared and armed to the teeth. At the bar stood three women who were obviously prostitutes and looked as tough and uncouth as the men. In the midst of this motley, unclean, hard drinking crowd—not one of whom had probably ever heard of England, let alone Shakespeare—standing on the bar with incredible dramatic presence, was the man with that golden voice.

He was of medium height, no longer young, yet still strikingly handsome. His hair was curly and still jet black despite the deep wrinkles in his face. He sported a gallant mustache which gave him the look of a dandy and his manners where clearly those of a classical actor of the highest caliber. His presence was astonishing: the way he held himself, his graceful gestures, the smallest movement of his head. None of these were artificial or strained in any way.

But it was his eyes that made the most stunning impression. I will never forget them. They radiated, in a most haunting way, the tortured nature of his soul. Dark and melancholic, they seemed to shoot flames of fire into space, always focused inward and completely unaware of the grim surroundings. The words he spoke with such unmatched skill were no longer Macbeth's. They were his own. I knew immediately that his life was somehow as stained as the Nordic king whom he was portraying for no one but himself. I had never before, nor since, witnessed a human being so consumed by the shadows of a dark past.

Entranced by this unexpected and mystifying sight, I sat at one of the tables and watched the performance. I alone gave attention to the man standing on the bar. It was as though the two of us were in a different world separated by invisible walls and infinite space from those around us. This was without question the most bizarre experience of my life even though I had made it my goal to place myself in unusual situations. Nothing compared to this. Outside, the tumbleweed scratched against the door and the wind sent desert sands whirling into the room. The people were motionless, as dry and silent as the oceans of prairie surrounding them. They were like statues placed on a stage to create the most outlandish mismatch conceivable. One of the Mexican banditos let out a loud burp. But the man reciting Shakespeare kept on, paying no attention to his uncouth audience.

Suddenly a cold shiver shook my body from head to foot. His

dark eyes fell upon me and locked into mine. They pierced into my very soul. There was such gloom in them, and such pain.

With an old actor's flourish, the man spit out the Bard's poetry as though each word burned his innards.

"O, my offense is rank, it smells to heaven;
It hath the primal eldest curse upon't,
A brother's murder. Pray can I not,
Though inclination be as sharp as will.
My stronger guilt defeats my strong intent,
And like a man to double business bound
I stand in pause where I shall first begin,
And both neglect. What if this cursed hand
Were thicker than itself with brother's blood,
Is there not rain enough in the sweet heavens
To wash it white as snow? Whereto serves mercy
But to confront the visage of offense?
And what's in a prayer but this twofold force,
To be forestalled ere we come to fall,
Or pardoned being down? Then I'll look up.
My fault is past. But, O, what form of prayer
Can serve my turn? "Forgive me my foul murder"?
O wretched state! O bosom black as death!
O limed soul, that struggling to be free
Art more engaged! Help, angels! Make assay."

During the soliloquy, the man took several swigs from the bottle and continued on without missing a beat. His eyes were aflame with the theatrics that make actors famous, but there was also something desperate about him. He was a man whose soul had been in agonizing pain for many years.

The audience hardly noticed that he had finished his performance. He stared at them with disdain, taking another drink to smother the humiliation. The sound of one pair of hands clapping suddenly broke through the noise of the crowd. The strange actor interrupted his drinking and looked out into the shadows, surprised. Unable to help myself, I stood and continued to applaud, ignoring my neighbor's complaints.

The actor bowed with a sarcastic sneer and stumbled off the bar. He made his way to an empty table and collapsed in a chair. I decided to approach him.

"What are you looking at, boy?"

"Forgive me, sir. I...I didn't mean to..."

"Sit down and join me for a drink."

"Thank you, sir," I muttered nervously.

The man placed the bottle in the center of the table and looked around for a glass. Seeing none, he called to the bartender.

"A glass for my young friend, Smitty!"

"I'm fine, sir. I don't drink."

"You're joking. What kind of man doesn't indulge?"

"I'm a preacher's son, sir."

The man suddenly became suspicious. I searched my pockets and pulled out a silver dollar. I was saving it for the next stage of my journey. I would have to wire my father from Tucson as San Francisco still lay far off.

He poured himself a shot glass and lifted it to his lips. I noticed a slight tremble in his fingers as he threw it back and swallowed the liquor in one gulp. His face reddened while it burned a path to his stomach. The windburned features softened as a wave of release swept over him. It was clear to me that he was seeking the temporary relief of that secret pain which ate at him relentlessly.

His aquiline nose bore the marks of too many shotglasses across too many years. Purple snake-like blood vessels marred a once noble nose. The eyes were forever bloodshot, hazy with melancholy and alcohol. This was the face of a broken spirit and though he could still roar his way through the golden verse of the great bard, his life after the performance was a tragic shambles heading in only one direction—the grave.

He turned his dark eyes upon me with a glare of anger.

"You're observing me, boy."

"I'm sorry, sir," I said, faltering beneath his condemning look.

"Observation is a good thing. Every artist must employ it. I've done it for a lifetime. But the observer is often one who does not like to be watched in turn."

"Are you a professional actor, sir?"

The gallant drunkard poured himself another shot and drank it as though he was in urgent need of putting out some hidden fire.

"I'll ask you what you are, son. You're surely no cowpoke."

"I'm wanting to be a writer," I said with pride.

"A writer?" he cried out as his eyes widened with interest. "What kind of a writer?"

"Well, I hope to work for a paper back East and then, someday, I'd like to pen a novel."

"That's good, that's very good. So you're out to see the world, to fetch your material?"

"I guess you could say that."

"Full of curiosity, eh?" he said with a strange twinkle.

I shook my head, uncertain as to whether this revelation would make him gunshy.

He stared at me intently. His tired eyes took on a hawk-like glaze which must have once graced his youthful brow. He took the bottle in his hands with almost loving affection.

"I'll make a bargain with you, young man. You keep me stocked with this devil's brew and I'll give you a story the like of which you've never heard before."

I felt a shiver shoot through my entire body, as though I had discovered some mysterious treasure, some secret cave packed with wonders lost out here on the far side of untamed wilderness.

"Do we have an agreement?"

"You have my word."

"You must also swear on whatever is holy to you that you won't write a word until I'm dead, which can't be too far off now."

I nodded and studied his features more carefully. I could see that his face had the reddish puffiness of the hopeless drinker whose health has long been left behind and whose future was assured. Only the coffin nails would manage to separate him from his poison. But there was still enough of a shred of dignity left in his behavior to make him interesting. And there was still enough life in him to radiate the icy breeze of a desperate melancholy which would never be healed. Something dreadful had wrecked his life and left him a broken hull carried helplessly by the ocean waves of life.

After placing another silver dollar on the table as proof of my commitment to our agreement, he rose and adjusted the rags of a gentleman fallen on hard times.

"Let's take a walk, friend," he stated with a courteous but slurring voice. "This den of iniquity is too oppressive for my soul."

I followed him out into the hot sun, noticing a distinctive limp which had nothing to do with the alcohol he had imbibed. I wondered what story lay behind his crippled leg—an old war wound perhaps? He was of the generation which had fought in that dread-

ful nightmare drifting over our country's recent past, the so-called
Civil War.

We stepped out into the afternoon sun. My head swirled as
the brilliant desert light flooded my vision. My companion pulled
out a large scarf of exotic design and color from his pocket and
swiftly wrapped it around his head. Though I had never seen such
a cloth, I recognized it as a creation from far-off Asia. His skill in
using it to protect himself against the merciless sun further convinced me that he had once lived in some foreign land.

I walked alongside him down the dirt path which must have
been considered Main Street in this desolate town. I didn't have
the vaguest notion where we were headed, but I sensed that something of great import was about to be unveiled.

The mysterious gentleman limped toward the hotel, the only
one within two hundred miles. It was named "the Grand Hotel"
which was someone's idea of a joke since the building was as ordinary as the barns silhouetted on all corners of the horizon.

My companion acknowledged the front desk clerk in a gesture
that had long become habit. I followed him up a creaking stairway
to his room. He threw open the door and turned to me for the first
time since we had left the saloon.

"Welcome to my castle, Milord!"

He bowed theatrically and motioned for me to enter. The room
was barren with only a bed, desk, and chest of drawers to fill the
emptiness. The walls were utterly denuded of any decor. A pale,
yellowish paper hid the wood from the eye. Water stains spotted
the room, along with the outline of frames which had once
attempted to beautify this wretched space.

"Sit!" the old gentleman ordered, sending the one chair in the
room over to me.

I sat as he pulled off his scarf and threw the window open. He stared out at the cloudless sky with the intensity of a ship captain peering out over a vast horizon.

"Soon..." he whispered.

I wanted to ask him what he meant, but the tone of his voice had such an anguish to it that I restrained my curiosity. He took a deep breath and let it out slowly.

"I killed a man once..."

A shiver shook me so that my hands involuntarily gripped the arms of the chair.

"Killed him while his back was to me!"

His words carried a quiver of unspeakable guilt. I could no longer tell if I was breathing or not.

"I never was much of a believer...But there's one thing I've come to know. I've got the Curse of Cain on me!"

"The Curse of Cain?" I asked, not being well read in the good book.

"Behold, thou hast driven me this day away from the face of the earth and I shall be a fugitive and a wanderer in the earth..."

I sat in silence, feeling the weight of his great pain.

"I thought they'd call me a hero, boy," he stated slowly as he turned toward me. His eyes glistened with tears. "And look at me...A drunkard lost on the furthest edge of civilization!"

He snickered strangely.

"I was applauded by hundreds and hundreds of people once. You find that hard to believe, don't you?"

He took a step forward and held up his arms toward the cracks in the ceiling.

"I was a prince of the stage! I was hailed as the greatest of my day!"

He turned a glazed look upon me.

"I've died more times than I can remember on the stage. And now that I really want to die, I can't seem to be able to do it."

I didn't know what to say. I wanted to ease his pain but it was obviously far too late.

"I've wandered in lands you've never heard of, son. I've lived in places you wouldn't leave your dog in..."

Then his voice lowered to a whisper.

"I've been lonelier than the loneliest human being ever to walk upon this earth."

He pulled out a medicine vial from the desk drawer and opened it slowly.

"I have longed for this day...for nearly forty years. But I needed a witness...Someone to have pity on me..."

He emptied the vile in one swallow, made a terrible grimace, then looked at me with a strange peace in his melancholic eyes.

"You are that man...I beg of you, do not find me a doctor when the poison takes effect. For know that this is my punishment."

I jumped to my feet, horrified.

"My God, man, what have you done?"

"I have killed a man. A man named Abraham Lincoln...I am John Wilkes Booth!"

He slumped to the floor, grasping his sides as the poison burned his stomach. It would take three days for him to die. If there is a Hell, he had found it long before meeting his Maker.

PICTORIAL

John Wilkes Booth's Daughter
Ogarita
(1860 - 1892)

John Wilkes Booth's wife
Izola Mills D'Arcy

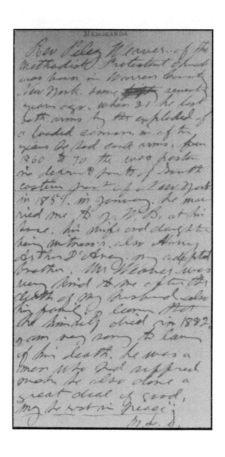

From Izola's diary;
"Rev. Peleg Weaver, of the Methodist Protestant Church, was born in Warren County, New York, some seventy years ago. . . In 1859, in January, he married me to J.W.B. at his house, his wife & daughter being witnesses, also Harry Arthur D'Arcy, my adopted brother."

Izola Forrester, author of
"This One Mad Act"

Beatrice Colony, the author's
great - grandmother

John Wilkes Booth's son, Harry Stevenson
(Born in 1870, conceived during the brief reunion of John Wilkes Booth and Izola.)

*Junius Brutus Booth,
John Wilkes Booth's famous
father*

*Edwin Booth,
John Wilkes Booth's
brother*

*Mary Ann Holmes Booth,
John Wilkes Booth's mother*

A Family Tree

Booth

Beatrice, John Wilkes Booth's
granddaughter

Ogarita, John Wilkes Booth's
daughter

*Charles Edward Clutts,
the author's grandfather*

*Patricia Anne, the author's
mother*

Theodore J. Nottingham

Theodore Nottingham　　　　*John Wilkes Booth*

Strange, indeed, it is to contemplate the results of that old tragedy. It is like the way in which Nature, in her resistless course, wipes out the vestiges of ancient wars and civilizations, with new growth -- green trees and flowers over ruins and graves. There is no shadow of horror or danger reaching out to John Wilkes Booth's descendants. There is merely a heritage of dramatic inclination, and a flair for the romantic, and once in a while a child is born with the wide ox-like dark eyes of brooding intensity. Then, we say, that one has the Booth look.

Izola Forrester
This One Mad Act

PART TWO

THE LEGACY

THE DESCENDANTS

Booth had one daughter, Ogarita, who bore two girls, Beatrice and Izola. Beatrice was my great-grandmother. Her sister Izola grew up to be a fine writer and the author of the book *This One Mad Act.*

Both sisters were attracted to the theater, and Beatrice went on to manage a summer theater in Keene, New Hampshire to the very end of her life. Our family recently uncovered a few autobiographical pages that she wrote, reflecting on the world of her youth. Several paragraphs are published here for the first time, as they express something of the Booth legacy passed on through the generations.

These are the words of Beatrice Colony, granddaughter of John Wilkes Booth:

My earliest recollections are centered around the theatre, for both my parents were "troupers". I happened to be born in Chicago, where my father was directing the Gilbert and Sullivan operas, during the winter season of 1885; and my mother laid off long enough for my advent into the world, in a furnished room on West Madison Street. My sister, Izola, has often told me of her surprise on returning from school at noon, to find a fat, red-faced baby holding the place of honor, and hearing mama say, "Isn't she beautiful, Zola?" I gather that her reactions were a bit uncertain as to the beauty of the fat, wriggling sister then, but in all the years of difficulties, struggles and happy go-lucky vagabondage which went with trouping in those days, there has never been any doubt about her devotion to that same sister.

Having the same heritage of the Booths, there has always been a great bond, that neither time nor space, bad luck or good fortune, can sever. I can't remember when I did not know there was a mystery in the family concerning the handsome grandfather, John Wilkes Booth, and that I must never speak of him. My memories are too vague concerning the period before my mother's death, when I was eight years old, to write about—only the highlights seem to stand out.

That cold, deadly spring of one night stands through New York state, when I was playing children's parts with my mother doing "leads" will always seem a horror to me, for all at once I was sent to New York with one of the actors who was leaving the company. I looked back from the door of the little hotel room at my mama lying there, so still and white and sick, with her short curly hair brushed back from her face. A few days later, I was told by my uncle Harry Stevenson, that mama was gone and would not be back. He was really just a youngster himself—around eighteen or so, and he adored my mother. We seemed so alone and frightened. She is buried there in Binghampton, where she passed on, leaving two little girls to carry on the torch of accomplishment.

Zola was in Chicago, where she had been boarding with Mr. and Mrs. George Forrester, who adopted her after mama died. Although we were half-sisters, having the same mother seemed to make us very near and close to each other. In many ways, she was more fortunate than I, for wherever she was left, she seemed to land on her feet, and had the advantage of the sort of education which fitted her for her career as a writer.

There is something about the theatre which, once in the blood, hold ever and always a call which is impossible to still. I have been in and out of the theatre all my life, and worked at many things, but always turn back to the call of the blood. Generations of actors rise up within you, urging you on and on to give of yourself to a great art. It doesn't matter whether you make any money out of it or not, but every so often, you must act.

My grandfather, Charles Edward Clutts, Beatrice's son, also grew up under the shadow of the Booth tragedy. He felt that in his day, it was still dangerous to let it be known that he was related to Booth. His childhood was shattered by the wandering life of the acting troupe to which his mother Beatrice belonged. My mother, Patricia Anne, eldest child of Charles Edward Clutts, appeared in a couple of plays at the summer theater in Keene, New Hampshire under the direction of her grandmother Beatrice Booth Colony. It seems to me that the Booth legacy carried its consequences down through some of these lives by enveloping them in a mist of restlessness that nothing could satisfy. My own experience was a clear reflection of this phenomenon.

For years, I traveled back and forth between two continents, seeking to express the theatrical gifts I had inherited and that forced me on relentlessly against all logic.

I carried with me a picture of my ancestor because I felt such a kinship with him. Not only was my blood boiling with the legacy of his creative skills and dramatic inclinations, but the dark side of his destiny seemed to cast its shadow on my life. In a way, my experience as a descendant of John Wilkes Booth is a metaphor for the experiences all people hold in common: Each of us inherit characteristics, inclinations, and the effects of ancient causes.

This saga is more than the fate of a family enveloped in the dark deed of a zealous ancestor. This is a story of crime and punishment, mystery and tragedy, and finally redemption and new beginning.

BOOTH'S DAUGHTER

My great-aunt Izola Forrester described her memories of her mother, Booth's daughter, in her book *This One Mad Act*:

My mother could remember her father and the thrill of reunion and happiness throughout the family. She would sit on her father's knee at the table, and be petted and noticed until it was bedtime. There seemed to be a succession of arrivals and departures throughout these early misty years. Sometimes it would be her mother, young and tense and eager, kissing and embracing her in farewell, and driving away for long mysterious absences. Again there would come an unexpected moment when she would find herself arrayed in her daintiest frock, and she would be taken by her mammy down to a candle-lit room, to find her father with her mother at home again.

And always, around these early memories, there was the impression of danger; of distant cannon rolling like rumbling thunder in the mountains, and puffs of smoke rising from the wooded heights and river bottoms. One day, my mother opened a long narrow box and showed me its contents for the first time. There was the medallion I knew well; but I had not been allowed before to press its secret spring myself, and see what lay beneath the blue backing, behind my sister's picture. It was a curl of heavy, black hair. My mother told me that it was a lock of my grandfather's hair. It lay pressed against a small oval photograph of him.

My mother had been named Ogarita Rosalie. I often wondered why she was so quiet and aloof in manner. "Few friends and no confidantes," she would say when she told me never to discuss our family with anyone. It made me realize again that peculiar wall of separation which seemed to shut us off from other people, and concerned my grandfather. I must never speak of him to strangers, I was warned, and never answer any questions concerning him.

John Wilkes Booth's daughter died of pneumonia at age thirty-two. An obituary in *The New York World* from April 15, 1892 left this testimonial:

"*Wilkes Booth's Daughter.*

Rita Booth, Character Actress and wife of Albert Henderson is dead.

Rita Booth, who is said to have been the daughter of Wilkes Booth, the slayer of President Lincoln, died on Tuesday, in Binghamton, N.Y., where she had been playing in the company of Floy Crowell...

Rita Booth was a clever character actress, and often declared that she did not wish to rise to any eminence in the dramatic profession, because she feared her relationship would bring her unpleasant notoriety. She wore always a medallion locket containing the likeness of the ill-fated John Wilkes Booth.

Several people who knew Booth claimed to have noted in her the clear-cut features, the big ox eyes, the curly hair and high brow of the man who was regarded as the rising actor of his time. It is a chapter of dramatic history that ought not to be lost."

BOOTH'S SON

Izola Forrester left us these words in memory of Harry Jerome Henderson:

The strongest proof of the escape, to me, is Booth's son, Harry. No one who had ever known him could question the relationship. Even strangers, all during his life, observed the resemblance and commented on it, to his everlasting embarrassment and unhappiness. He was not proud of the fact that he was Booth's son. He dreaded being connected or involved with the tragic circumstances around the assassination, just as my mother did. It was an ever-present menace, that people might find out they were the children of the assassin of Lincoln. Whether, so far as she was concerned, this feeling died away, I cannot say, but during the last three years of her life, she wore his picture openly in the old medallion brooch at her throat.

To the end of his life, Harry remained a gentleman drifter. He would spend his last quarter for a volume of poems from a stand outside a second-hand book shop along Fourth Avenue, and gloat over his prize, while it meant cutting out his next meal. He would part with anything he owned to help a friend, and he had many friends, some of them the strangest friends any man ever won to himself.

He was forty-eight when he died. I remember the day of his funeral. As the world looks at it, he was a failure. He never could earn money, or keep it. He had led, for years, the life of a modern wandering minstrel. They used to call him around the old Tenderloin resorts and the lesser variety theatres, the "man of a thousand songs."

He was known from Harlem down to the Bowery. He would drop into a place, and sing a few songs, picking up a dollar or more here and there, and probably giving it away to those he considered needed it more than he did before the night was gone.

At his funeral, an old fellow said, tears rolling unashamed down his cheeks: "Everybody loved Harry. There was some of us who thought we knew who he was, but he never talked about it. One night down in McCoy's saloon, an old Southerner said to him that he looked exactly like John Wilkes Booth and Harry just stared at him, and bowed, and said he must be mistaken."

Harry Stevenson was a strange personality, combining all of the attributes of the beloved vagabonds of the world, with the mystery of his birth marooning him for life in a no-man's land of human existence.

DOWN THROUGH
THE GENERATIONS

Throughout my youth, I felt particularly drawn to the twenty-six year old matinee idol whose destiny was aborted by the most horrific of acts. I too was drawn early on to the theater and thereby felt a sort of genetic connection with the Booths who in their day were the premiere American family of the theater.

For years, I heard the tale of the murder, of the "insane" lone actor, of the epic manhunt, and of the final capture and death scene. The drama of my family's destiny is closely tied to the events that took place at the time of the assassination. The need for secrecy, the agony carried on for generations, and the fierce loyalty to a vanished person became part of the lives of those who followed in the wake of Booth's tragic choice.

Along with the inherited attraction to the theater, some of us seem to have been showered with a certain restless wanderlust, as though the ancient curse that fell so heavily upon my ancestor was still working itself out.

In my case, destiny sent me to Europe and I grew up as a man without a country. Then in my early twenties, I traveled a great deal in search of that vague mirage called Truth. Like some other descendants of the Booths, I was drawn to the esoteric and the mystical. In fact, this became my passion as I sought out meaning and purpose.

My great-grandmother, Booth's granddaughter, had published a book of mystical poetry and was involved for many years with the Rosicrucians. This particular fancy for the more hidden side of things may well be what led John Wilkes Booth into the Masonic secrecies of the Knights of the Golden Circle. The consequences, we believe, were disastrous for everyone. Yet, behind the mystery and the drama, lies a human soul seeking understanding and wisdom. Booth was not able to find it in the midst of the madness of the Civil War.

My own wanderings took me to Asia. The winds of the South China Sea and the aroma of incense burning at roadside shrines spoke to me of spiritual transformation. Having lived in the noise and frantic pace of the West's great capitals, I now discovered the deep peace that opens onto enlightenment. For the first time, the dark intensity of the Booth inheritance gave way to the clarity of being present to a world not limited by the affairs of human beings.

Here I found what John Wilkes Booth had failed to uncover in his life. The madness of war and politics, ambition and limelight faded away beneath the joy of being part of a greater Life, the one spoken of by sages and saints of all centuries. In this awareness, hatred gives way to forgiveness, selfishness to compassion. The winter of melancholy melts before the spring of spiritual awakening and the realization that we are all connected to the unfathomable universal life.

THE LAST CHAPTER

But there is one more chapter to this story. One that seems to bring things full circle for my family and the burden of its legacy.

It takes place in the town of Enid out in the Oklahoma plains.

The year was 1903. A strange man had taken residence in the Grand Hotel in this dusty town at the edge of barren wilderness. He was known to have traveled from other lost places in the Southwest, spouting Shakespeare and guzzling whiskey.

Twice, he lay on what he thought to be his death bed and shared with a clergyman the dark secret he carried with him. This mysterious man, called by some John Saint Helen and by others David E. George, confessed that he was none other than John Wilkes Booth. Upon recovery, he would vanish deeper into the desert plains.

The end of the road for his painful, lonely journey would be Enid, Oklahoma. There, on the edge of civilization and far from loved ones and friends, the man poisoned himself. The local farmers were so sure of his identity as the President's assassin that they wanted to hang him even as he lay dying. So ended the life of a man cursed with Cain's burden.

Eighty years later, knowing nothing of this story of misery and desolation, I came to Enid, Oklahoma. I was there to fulfill the vocation that had taken hold of me. I was there to attend seminary and enter into Christian ministry.

This place that was the end of the road for my ancestor myste-riously became the beginning of my life's journey. I was married there and my daughter was born at the local hospital, not far from where the Grand Hotel had once stood. This was the place where I came out of the darkness of my own life of searching and melan-choly. We had driven there directly from Hollywood, California where my ancestral inclinations had sought to follow in the old family tradition.

I had found a new direction, one that broke me away from the shadow of Booth's influence in my life. New life was born on the very ground where the old life had sadly withered away. Like the magic of spring, new possibilities flowered where once death reigned supreme.

It has taken four or five generations to come out of the shadow cast by Booth's mad act. Whether he was shot at the barn, or escaped, or ended his days in a desolate town, justice had the last word. But his legacy has continued to haunt the children that have come after him. Here too, justice has shown its light. The inheri-tance of tragedy has taught us to turn our efforts toward handing down a legacy of goodness and right action in the world. This is the secret of turning such a curse into a blessing.

PART THREE

THE RESEARCH

INTRODUCTION

Every American who lived in 1865 knew of the strange actions which panicked government officials took when they chased after the President's murderer. Every American knew that something was wrong, that the Secretary of War was veiling the burial of the captured corpse, that the Congressional Committee called the Head of the Secret Service a liar. It was a time of terrible disorder in a country still smoldering with rebellion, and the government's only way to appease the people was to catch a man as fast as possible. Why, then, do these historians take the government's statements as fact when no one did in 1865? Is it a lack of comprehension? A laziness to dig up the ugly truth? A refusal to question the loyalty and honesty of government officials?

Let us temporarily close our eyes to the indoctrination we have been fed since our grade school teachers opened the history book to the Civil War Era and the easy stereotypes of crazed, lone assassins which simplified the task of understanding why the gun was fired. We must now open our minds to the possibilities that some historians have failed to notice because of blind acceptance of a quickly shut case, or because of a reluctance to tread in the muck of pay-offs, betrayal and deceit.

1
WHO WAS HE?

John Booth's father was the uncontested premiere actor of the American stage. Junius Brutus Booth came to the New World in 1821 and traveled the country exciting audiences with thundering performances of Shakespeare's classics. One of his many admirers was Walt Whitman, who said of him: "His genius was to me one of the grandest revelations of my life, a lesson of artistic expression."

John's brother Edwin followed in his father's steps and became the reigning master of his craft with his legendary portrayal of Hamlet during one hundred consecutive nights at New York's Winter Garden theater.

John's fame came quickest of all. He took to the stage at the age of seventeen and soon was a sensation from Richmond to Boston. When he opened as Richard the Third at Grover's Theatre on April 11, 1863, he was billed as: "The Pride of the American people—The youngest tragedian in the world—a star of the first magnitude—son of the great Junius Brutus Booth—Brother and artistic rival of Edwin Booth."

The newspapers of the day hailed him as a "complete triumph." A critic of the day wrote: "His youth, originality, and superior genius have not only made him popular but established him in the hearts of Washington people as a great favorite." Fellow actors said that he possessed "extraordinary presence and magnetism."

He was universally considered the most handsome man to grace the stage. "He was the idol of women" said British actor Charles Wyndham. Lady Anne Hartley Gilbert observed that he was "a very handsome man, perhaps the handsomest I ever saw."

The *Washington Chronicle* announced that "this handsome, passionate boy as an actor has more of the native fire and fury of his great father than any of his family...He has more of the old man's power in one performance than Edwin can show in a year." The *Boston Daily Advertiser* called him "the greatest actor in the country" and the *Baltimore Sun* proclaimed: "an actor with the suddenness of a meteor now illuminates the dramatic horizon."

Backstage, a colleague said of him, echoing the sentiments of many fellow actors: "He was the gentlest man I ever knew. In rehearsal, he was always considerate of the other actors, and if he had a suggestion to make, he always made it with the utmost courtesy."

John Booth and his sister Asia were best friends and she remembered him as cheerful, joyful, fun loving. "Let us not be sad," her brother Johnny would say to her, "life is so short, and the world so beautiful. Just to breathe is delicious."

She tells of a moment on their father's farm in Maryland, when she caught a katydid and wanted to keep it for her collection. John responded: "No you don't, you bloodthirsty female. Katy shall be free and shall sing tonight on in the sycamores." In her diary, she wrote that he kissed the creature and placed it on a tree leaf.

Together, they read verses and sang, and he taught her to ride horses.

"How glorious it is to live!" she remembered her younger

brother saying.

Asia Booth also recounts the day when a strange event cast a shadow on the happy life of her vivacious playmate. A Gypsy fortune teller had read his palm.

"Ah, you've a bad hand, the lines all criss-cross. It's full enough of sorrow—full of trouble—trouble in plenty, everywhere I look. You'll break hearts, they'll mean nothing to you. You'll die young and leave many to mourn you, many to love you too, but you'll be rich, generous, and free with your money. You're born under an unlucky star. You've got in your hand a thundering crowd of enemies—not one friend—you'll make a bad end, and have plenty to love you afterwards. You'll have a fast life—short, but a grand one.

"I've never seen such a worse hand, and I wish I hadn't seen it, but every word I've told is true by the signs. You'd best turn a missionary or priest and try to escape it."

2
THE POLITICAL SETTING

Washington D.C., April 14, 1865

To My Countrymen:

For years I have devoted my time, my energies, and every dollar I possess in the world to the furtherance of an object. I have been baffled and disappointed. The hour has come when I must change my plan. Many, I know—the vulgar herd—will blame me for what I am about to do, but posterity, I am sure, will justify me. Right or wrong, God judge me, not man. Be my motive good or bad, of one thing I am sure, the lasting condemnation of the North...This war is a war with the constitution and the reserve rights of the state. It is a war upon southern rights and institutions. The nomination of Abraham Lincoln four years ago bespoke the war. His election forced it. I have ever held the South was right. In a foreign war I too could say, "country, right or wrong." But in a struggle such as ours (where brother tries to pierce the brother's heart) for God's sake choose the right.

People of the North, to hate tyranny, to love liberty and justice, to strike at wrong and oppression was the teaching of our fathers. The study of our early history will not let me forget it, and may it never...

I do not want to forget the heroic patriotism of our fathers, who rebelled against the oppression of mother country...The South are not, nor have they been, fighting for the continuance of slavery. The first battle of Bull Run did away with that idea. Their causes for the war have been as noble and greater far than those that urged our fathers on. Even should we allow that they were wrong at the beginning of the contest, cruelty and injustice have made the wrong become the right, and they stand now before the wonder and admiration of the world as a noble band of patriotic heroes. Hereafter, reading of their deeds Thermopylae will be forgotten...

I have studied hard to discover upon what grounds the right of a state to secede has been denied, whether our very name, United States, and the Declaration of Independence provide for secession. But there is now no time for words...I love justice more than I do a country that disowns it; more than fame and wealth; more (heaven pardon me if wrong) more than a happy home...Four years ago I would have given a thousand lives to see her (the United States) remain (as I had always known her) powerful and unbroken, and now I would hold my life as naught to see her what she was. Oh! my friends, if the fearful scenes of the past four years had never been enacted, or if what has been had been a frightful dream, from which we could now awake, with what overflowing hearts could we bless our God and pray for his continual favor...

Heartsick and disappointed I turn from the path which I have been following into a bolder and more perilous one. Without malice I make the change. I have nothing in my heart except a sense of duty to my choice. If the South is to be aided it must be done quickly...

He who loves his country better than gold or life,

John W. Booth (5)

When the news of Lincoln's assassination began to spread

across the country, people ran out of their houses—many of them dancing with joy. Though Booth has been tagged with the image of the lone maniac, the insane, evil-eyed killer, his act was purely a political matter which many openly condoned. The South, of course, was overjoyed, although most came to realize that they had lost their best friend. Lincoln was one of the few Northerners who wanted to patch things up as soon as possible. Forgive and forget was his philosophy. And men whose hearts were not big enough for such compassion were the happiest of all when the President was shot. The Radical Republicans wanted to kick the South mercilessly now that it was on its knees. Lincoln was in hostile territory whether north or south of the Mason-Dixon Line.

There were many plots to assassinate the President (6). A Southern gentleman even advertised a reward in a newspaper for ten thousand dollars to anyone who did the job. And there was a secret organization which was tightly sewn throughout the defeated states called the Knights of the Golden Circle, a mysterious, militant branch of Freemasonry.

THE KNIGHTS OF THE GOLDEN CIRCLE

Like many politically active Southerners, John Wilkes Booth belonged to the order in his home city, Baltimore (7). In the State, War and Navy Building in Washington D.C. a visitor can find a little octagonal tin star lying amidst Booth's relics. On the fly-leaf of a small Book of Common Prayer is written a secret cipher which was used as evidence in the Conspiracy Trial showing that Booth had been on special duty with John H. Surratt between Richmond and Canada (8).

This society's hushed existence has always been one of the

spell-binding details of the Civil War. Under the names of the Sons of Liberty and the Order of American Knights, this invisible organization claimed a membership of over three hundred thousand (9).

The official report to Washington in March, 1865 reads: "There existed in the Northern States an essentially military organization known as the Sons of Liberty, whose principle was that the States were sovereign, and that there was no authority in the Central Government to coerce a seceding state. It was estimated that the total membership of this society was fully 300,000 of which 85,000 resided in Illinois, 50,000 in Indiana and 40,000 in Ohio (10)."

This secret society operated under other names as well—the Peace Party, the Constitutional Party, the American Legion—and had large groups in Canada and Europe. Their main organ of communication was a New York paper called *The Caucasian*. They also controlled *The New York Herald, The Journal of Commerce, Express, The Courier* (a French paper), *The Post* in Boston, *The Times* in Hartford, *The Atlas* and *The Argus* in Albany, *The Union* in Rochester, *The Courier* in Buffalo, *The Enquirer* in Cincinnati, *The Free Press* in Detroit, *The Times* in Chicago, *The News* in Milwaukee, and many less important ones. (11)

There were rumors that secret dispatches were sometimes intercepted by the Order and transmitted to rebel generals, causing terrible defeats to the Union forces. The formula from the ritual was: "If you go to the east, I will go to the west. Let there be no strife between mine and thine, for we be brethren." (12)

Thaddeus Stevens had accused the Order of instigating the assassination. The Secretary of War, who himself had declared that they were under the leadership of "those who cannot be reached" (13), was quoted in the newspapers the day after the crime, accusing them of being involved in the murder. For a least a year, the War Department conducted secret investigations on the motives and strength of this silent cloud that hovered from coast to coast. Certain men were arrested in Indiana, charged with being leaders of the Order: Stephen Horsey, Lambdin P. Milligan, and Dr. William A. Bowles. (14)

Tried in Indianapolis on Friday, May 19, 1865, they were sentenced to death by hanging. But at the last moment, they were reprieved by secret order of President Johnson and set free after the close of the war. (15)

The head of the Knights of the Golden Circle was found to be Brigadier-General George W. L. Bickley, head of the Secret Service of the Confederacy. When finally arrested, he was taken from prison to prison so that his friends would not discover his whereabouts. On March 5, 1865, Brigadier-General N. C. McLean wrote a letter to Brigadier-General Canby. In his conclusion, he states: "Bickley is evidently a very dangerous rebel of consummate ability, and perfectly unscrupulous in all respects. In my judgment he should never be released during the war, as I do not believe he can be controlled by any oath he might agree to take." (16)

In October, 1865, the secret prisoner of war was released from Fort Warren and disappeared in the impenetrable fog of sworn silence, secret rituals, and oaths of loyalty.

The Bickley dossier, the emblems of his Order, its great seal, its ritual and secret cipher code were included in the evidence used at the Conspiracy Trial. Yet they cannot be found in the records of the War Department, either in the Secret Service, or the Prisoner of War records. After the trial they were hidden away with Booth's relics, not to be uncovered until 1932 when Izola

Forrester, the granddaughter of John Wilkes Booth who spent forty years researching the plight of her infamous relative, was allowed to descend to the basement of the old State, War and Navy Building and unlock the trunk containing exhibits from the Trial. (17)

It is obvious that the Secretary of War was still carrying out his first accusation, especially since it was known that Booth was a member of the Order. According to Mrs. Forrester, her grand-mother (Booth's wife) talked of him as being the "tool of other men." (18) We may wonder why these extraordinary documents ended up in a locked trunk, officially forgotten until Lincoln's son had been buried. In our search to discover the mysteries surrounding the tragic murder, we must look further than the pistol that interrupted the laughter at Ford's Theater.

As complex, and perhaps as essential to our clues as the Knights of the Golden Circle, is the mind of one man who for a short while was the most powerful person in the United States of America—Secretary of War Edwin M. Stanton.

CONFLICTS WITH THE SECRETARY OF WAR

Abe Lincoln was beloved for his kindness. But the men on Capitol Hill felt he carried it too far. His Secretary of War was one of the most disagreeable men a president has ever had to work with. His contempt for the humorous Lincoln was open and unrestrained. Knowing that the President could not fire him in those crucial times, he actually tried to bend him to his wishes. In spite of, or because of the President's admiration and confidence in General McClellan, whom he wanted to make supreme commander of the Union Army, Secretary Stanton dismissed him. (19)

Edwin Stanton's neurotic behavior and hunger for power was a much discussed subject in the inner circles of Washington. Government officials could not decide whether the President simply did not mind Stanton's brutal manners or whether he hid his feelings beneath a mask of tolerant amusement. Whichever it may have been, Lincoln had the last word and his uncouth cabinet member was finally told who was the boss. As Otto Eisenchiml, the famed historian, put so well: "He had challenged the President and lost. It is possible that from then on Stanton's contempt was blended with hatred." (20)

3
THE ASSASSINATION

April 14, 1865. A few hours after sunset, one of America's greatest presidents would be slumped over in his box seat, a tiny hole in the back of his head. In testimony before a Congressional committee, Stanton stated at two different times that Lincoln never came to the War Department after April 13th. (21) But on that fateful day, the lanky man with the collar beard walked up the steps of the War Department. He had come to ask Stanton if Major Thomas Eckert could accompany him as bodyguard to Ford's Theater.

Major Eckert was a favorite of Mrs. Lincoln and a tough soldier, big enough to scare off a grizzly bear. But the Secretary of War refused on the grounds that he and Major Eckert had to work that evening. The telegraph operator, a man named Bates known for his honesty, published in 1907 that the President insisted on his request but that Stanton would not give in.

At nine-thirty that evening, a dispatch came to the War Department for President Lincoln. It was sent to the White House because the men on duty did not know that the President was watching *Our American Cousin*. Neither Stanton nor Eckert were there at the time! (22)

SET-UP FOR MURDER

It was in all the papers: Tonight Ulysses S. Grant and his wife would be accompanying the President to Ford's Theater to enjoy a performance starring Laura Keene. (23) The Secretary of War had also been invited but had refused. (24) According to the manager of the theater, there was never much of an attendance on Friday nights. But the unusual appearance of the colorful Supreme Commander had drawn a full house of curious admirers.

That night, however, as people entered the theater, they must have been sorely disappointed. Hardly any soldiers were present. When a general, let alone the Supreme Commander, comes to a public function, he is always accompanied by hordes of armed men. At the last moment, Grant had taken an evening train to go visit his children up north. (25) Even though he already had a strained relationship with Lincoln, he had suddenly changed his mind after accepting the presidential invitation. But the fact is that not even Ulysses S. Grant was that unmannered.

That afternoon the Secretary of War had come to see him and explained that going to the theater with the President would invite disaster. (26) Apparently Grant found this concern to be logical despite the fact that he played right into the hands of the murderers. Without Grant's escort for protection, and given a soldier on record for his unreliability (27), Abraham Lincoln was left entirely at the mercy of his enemies.

STRANGE OCCURRENCES

Within fifteen minutes, all telegraph wires around the city of Washington D.C. are severed (from 10:30 p.m. to 12:30 a.m.), except for a secret government wire which leads to Fort Old Point. Two wires in the main battery had been crossed and all service shorted. (28) Almost immediately, John Wilkes Booth's name is heard coming from the shouts of the hysterical crowd. Yet efforts are made to withhold his name from the press and for some hours after the assassination it is ruled out of military dispatches. (29)

By one in the morning of April 15th, his name is released. Alarms are sent to Winchester, Harper's Ferry, Cumberland, Baltimore, Annapolis, Acquia Creek, Relay House—but none go to the fat foot of Maryland which lies between the Potomac and the Patuxent where Booth is spurring on his horse. (30) The Port Tobacco road leading southward is left unguarded the entire night. (31)

THE CAPTORS

General James R. O'Beirne has been considered by historians as the one man to deserve the credit for discovering the route taken by Booth. Why did he not receive the credit officially? When O'Beirne thought he had cornered the fugitive, he sent a telegram to Washington reporting the direction they were headed and asked for orders. He was told to return to his command in Maryland. (32)

The final honors were given to Lieutenant Luther Baker, cousin of Lafayette C. Baker, the head of the Secret Service, along with Colonel Everton J. Conger, Major Edward P. Doherty and the twenty-two men of the 16th New York Regiment. The capture was taken from the hands of a first class general and put into those of two reward-hungry Secret Service detectives leading the most motley crew ever assembled to assist in a historical event. Thus began one of the strangest sagas of contradictions, exaggerations, mistakes, and lies ever produced in our history.

THE OFFICIAL VERSION

George Townsend, author of the government-sanctioned version of the capture, reported on the incident in the following words:

"The worn out horsemen retraced their steps, though some of them were so haggard and wasted with travel that they had to be kicked into intelligence before they could climb into their saddles." (34)

Testimony from both Lieutenant Baker and Colonel Conger states that the men fell off their horses and lay about in the grass asleep from exhaustion.

"Exhausted as the men were from having been in the saddle without sleep or rest since Monday night, instead of taking their stand to guard the rear and sides of the building, they dropped promiscuously under the trees, and it was with the utmost difficulty that Conger could prevail upon as few as six of their number to sit upon rails placed not less than thirty feet from the warehouse." (35)

In other words, it is two in the morning, sixteen men are sleeping in the grass, six are trying to keep their eyes open, and the three leaders are staring at a barn inside of which is one hundred thousand dollars worth of reward.

"The blaze lit up the black recesses of the great barn until every wasp's nest and cobweb in the roof was luminous, flinging streaks of red and violet across the tumbled gear in every corner, plows, harrows, hoes, rakes, sugar mills, and making every separate grain in the high bin adjacent, gleam like a mote of precious gold. They tinged the beams, the upright columns, the barricades, where clover and timothy, pilled high, held toward the hot incendiary their separate straws for the funeral pyre. They bathed the murderer's retreat in beautiful illumination, and while in bold outline his figure stood revealed, they rose like an impenetrable wall to guard from sight the hated enemy who lit them..." (36)

Townsend seems to have forgotten that it is April and that there is no hay in the barn that month. But more important, the building wasn't even a barn. It was a tobacco warehouse which, as the owner explained, held a few pieces of household furniture stored in a corner, and nothing else. (37)

As told in the history books, Private Boston Corbett finally ended the affair by shooting the man in the barn because he was told that the murderer was aiming at him (according to his testimony). (38) Robert Garrett, the twelve-year-old son of the farmer whose property was the scene of the killing, agrees that Corbett fired the fatal shot, but he adds that the soldier was only six feet from the barn and that the man inside never moved. He was visible because of a fire set by Conger who lit a small pile of brush that he had placed against the rear corner of the warehouse. (39)

This brings up the question of whether John Wilkes Booth was wanted dead or alive. The official orders were very clear: he was wanted alive. With sixteen hundred men on the chase, the largest manhunt in history, there was no reason why these orders could not be carried out. (40) Yet the detectives placed around Dr. Mudd's home, in case Booth returned, were ordered to shoot anyone who entered the garden. (41) As for Boston Corbett, no one is positive that he pulled the trigger. According to eye-witnesses, it was not until after Baker had demanded to know which member of the troop had disobeyed orders, and Conger had said he thought it had been suicide, that Corbett announced his deed. (42) A religious fanatic who had castrated himself after a night with prostitutes, Corbett said that God had directed him to do so. (43)

The real confusion does not begin until the dying man is brought out of the barn. According to the testimony of the Garrett family, the man dragged onto the porch was wearing a Confederate uniform. Townsend also agrees and adds that the Garretts never deviated from their first testimony that the man who had been brought to their house was a Confederate soldier named John Howard Boyd. (44)

However, Major Ruggles and Bainbridge, whom Booth had met as he crossed the Potomac River, said that he was wearing black. In an article in *The New York World*, Townsend explains that he must have changed clothes at Dr. Mudd's home. But Thomas A. Jones, who met Booth the day after he left the doctor' house, describes him as wearing black as well. (45)

The affidavits made by Colonel Pedgram and others who saw the actor's remains in Baltimore in 1869, testify that he was dressed in black and wearing a high riding boot. Two soldiers at the Garrett farm, Joseph Ziegen and Wilson D. Kenzie state in affidavits that the man shot in the barn was wearing a Confederate uniform and soldier's boots. In other words, John Wilkes Booth fled dressed in a black suit; did not change at Dr. Mudd's; was supposedly taken from the barn in a Confederate uniform; was placed on the battleship Montauk for examination dressed in a black suit.

And there is another matter: one of the assets of this man considered "the most handsome man in America" was his long, curly black hair. Testimony shows that the doctor who nursed the dying man on the Garrett porch cut off a lock of hair and gave it to a Miss Holloway, a visiting friend of the Garretts.

Later, on the Montauk, General Baker talks of chasing some young lady away who was trying to snip off some of the dead man's hair. At the undertaker's, the witnesses notice the long hair, and Miss Blanche Chapman, Booth's cousin, cuts some off and gives it to Mary Ann Booth, the actor's mother. (46) Yet, it is an accepted fact among all historians who have studied the episode, that the testimony at the trial is correct: Booth shaved off his mustache and cut his hair short at Dr. Mudd's house!

There are several conclusions to this fact. As we will discover later, many believe that there were three men in the barn: Booth, Herold, and a Confederate soldier who may have been initiated the same night as the actor into the Knights of the Golden Circle. There have been many dramatic dialogues written which were said to occur between the man in the barn and Lieutenant Baker in the various descriptions of the scene.

Conger, who was commended on the floor of the House of Representatives as the one member of the trio to have any regard for the truth, stated that the man in the barn spoke only three times: to ask who the captors were; to ask that Herold be allowed to come out; to ask that he be given a fighting chance for his life. (47) Some historians have tried to depict an insane actor arrogantly reciting Shakespearean lines as he savagely eyed the Union soldiers. It is quite possible that the man spoke to save time. Time for another man to escape.

John Garrett, in his testimony, said that he and his brother had slept in a corn crib near the barn before the soldiers came, to make sure that Booth and Herold did not steal the horses. After it was all over, no horse could be found on the Garrett farm, and it was necessary to get an old black man who lived nearby to provide a wagon that would take the remains to the ferry. (48)

"Brother Jack and I went to the barn and locked the door. Not being satisfied with that precaution, as there were doors that fastened on the inside, we concluded to sleep...nearby to guard our horses." (49) An interesting item which has seldom been brought up is that the barn had double doors on all four sides, and large windows in the upper story. Lieutenant Baker testified on June 20, 1867: "The barn was about fifty by sixty feet. Only one door of the barn was opened. The door opened looking towards the house." (50)

The third man never expected to die. He was just trying to save time for Booth's escape. Historians who have followed this theory believe that he was the man who came to warn the actor of the approaching regiment and remained with them.

CLUES LEFT BEHIND

John Wilkes Booth's watch, ring, chain, scarf-pin, crutch, and pipe were never found. (51) His field glasses were discovered nine miles from the farm and hidden in the room of Garrett's daughter. (52) The skeleton keys in Booth's relics are believed to have been those of the conspirator Atzerodt. The actor's own keys were never found. Booth's diary was discovered in the overcoat in the barn. Conger took it, said nothing of it, and left immediately for Washington to hand it over personally to Secretary Stanton. (53)

A portion of the diary reads as follows:

After being hunted like a dog through swamps and woods, I am here in despair. And why? For doing what Brutus was honored for. What made William Tell a hero.

And yet I, for striking down a greater tyrant than they ever knew, am looked upon as a common cutthroat. My action is purer than either of theirs. One hoped to be great, the other had not only his country's, but his own wrongs to avenge. I struck for my country and that alone.

A country that groaned beneath this tyranny and prayed for this end, and yet, now behold the cold hand they extend to me. God cannot pardon me if I have done wrong!

The very little I left behind to clear my name, the Government will not allow to be printed. So ends all. For my country I have given up all that makes life sweet and holy; brought misery on my family, and sure there is no pardon in Heaven for me since man condemns me so.

Though I have a great desire and almost a mind to return to Washington, and in a measure, clear my name—which I feel I can do—I do not repent the blow I struck. I may before my God, but not to man. I think I have done well.

I am abandoned, with the curse of Cain upon me, when if the world knew my heart, that one blow would have made me great, though I desire no greatness.

Who can read this fate? God's will be done. I have too great a soul to die like a criminal. Oh, may He spare me that, and let me die bravely.

I bless the entire world. I have never hated nor wronged anyone. This last was not a wrong, unless God deems it so. And it is with him to damn or bless me. I do not wish to shed a drop of blood, but I must fight the course. Tis all that is left me.

Townsend stated that "none of the party who captured him were sure of his identity." (54) Even the historian Philip Van

Doren Stern, who upholds the official version of Booth's death, writes: "Such matters as the possibility of Booth's survival, or the exact manner of his death are unimportant in comparison with some of the still unsolved mysteries surrounding Lincoln's death." (55)

The dying man dragged onto the Garrett porch lived for three and a half hours. There have been accounts of his bravado and theatrical phrasing. But Theodore Roscoe, author of *The Web of Conspiracy*, one of the most in-depth books on the subject, disagrees. "We are only certain that a man agonized by a punctured spinal cord does not utter stilted speeches in the best tradition of Victorian literature." (56)

In all that time, no one tried to get information from the dying but conscious man. Stranger still is the fact that Major Doherty's interrogation of the captured David Herold during the time that the others were occupied with the man in the barn was never made known. It seems as if the gagging man on the blood-soaked porch was a mere puppet in the hands of his captors. He would say no more or less than they wanted him to. Nothing was to be uncovered at the Garrett farmhouse. They were only to capture a dead young man with black hair and a broken leg who was worth a fortune to his captors and a great appeasement to a frightened, unstable government.

In his postscript to *The Day Lincoln Was Shot*, Jim Bishop writes: "Booth was cornered in a Virginia barn and shot. For years afterwards there were stories that it wasn't Booth who was shot, but the stories were wrong. It was Booth..." (57)

In this way, the case was officially closed by all concerned, including future generations of history students. A last note on the capture episode. The body was thrown in a neighbor's old wagon and taken through the woods of rebel territory accompanied only by Lieutenant Baker and the Southern prisoner, Captain Jett, who had been forced into taking the troop to Booth's hideout. The other soldiers had gone by way of another route. For hours, the wagon disappeared in what some historians have called a blind spot in the story. When Baker re-appeared after his lone journey, Captain Jett had vanished. (58)

4
PROBLEMS OF IDENTIFICATION

SUSPICIOUS BEHAVIOR

A few people were brought onto the deck of the Montauk to identify the corpse. Among them was the photographer, Alexander Gardner, whose pictures, if he ever took any, were never released. (59) Heading the military commission whose purpose was to identify the body was a certain Major Eckert. (60)

The first observer was Seaton Monroe who immediately recognized the dead man by his general appearance. Several others, having seen Booth once or twice, agreed and went on record saying they had recognized him. Some mentioned the marks on his right hand.

Official word had been sent by the Provost Marshall General of Maryland, J. L. McPhail: "On his right hand are initials of his name, and on his left hand, between the forefinger and the thumb, a small cross, and across the same hand several spots, all in India ink." (61) These special marks were on his right arm. (61a)

Others said it was on his hand. Colonel Clarence Cobb, a good friend of Booth, was sent for by General Brice to help identify the body. But Surgeon-General J. K. Barnes told him that he was not needed. Junius Brutus Booth, the actor's father, was at a theater nearby, but was never summoned. (62)

Dr. Merrill, Booth's dentist, came on board with dental charts. The government was satisfied that the dental work "fully" identified the corpse. Yet, his testimony was never taken and is not on file. (63) Criminologists call the Coss-Uddengook Case the pioneer in dental identification and it took place in 1872, seven years later! (64)

Finally, Dr. Frederick May, a leading surgeon in Washington, was summoned. He had once performed an operation on John Wilkes Booth. In his report, the respected doctor writes: "The cover was removed, and to my great astonishment, revealed a body in whose lineaments there was to me no resemblance to the man I had known in life! My surprise was so great that I at once said to General Barnes, 'There is no resemblance in that corpse to Booth, nor can I believe it to be that of him.'" (65)

In the War Department Records, he testified that the man's face was freckled. Dr. May had ignored the first summons of the inquest. He was avowedly afraid of General Baker's men. (66)

However, the government had brought him to the Montauk to identify a scar which was left on Booth's neck from a surgical operation. With no professional exactitude, May described the area before seeing it. This became the greatest factor of identification—the "mark of the scalpel." It was not mentioned where the bullet hole was in relation to the scar. To quote Dr. May: "The scar looks as much like the effects of a burn as the cicatrix from a surgical operation. I recognize the likeness." (67)

The statement of Dr. Barnes, Surgeon-General of the United States, reads: "It looked like the scar of a burn instead of an incision." (68) Two years later, in a published essay, Dr. May referred to the broken leg of the corpse. He stated that it was the right leg.

(69) The actor who had jumped onto the stage on the night of April 14th had gotten his left spur caught in the overhanging flag.

CONFLICTING STORIES

General David A. Dana stated that he brought the body to Washington D.C. on the steamer John S. Ide, and buried it under a slab in the Navy Yard, hauling a battery of artillery over it.

Government detective William B. Wood testified that the body was taken from the steamer at the wharf on April 27; then taken by Baker and his nephew to an island twenty-seven miles out of Washington and buried there.

General Lew Wallace, Judge Advocate of the Conspiracy Trial, states: "To my personal knowledge the body was brought to Washington City, and buried in a room of the old brick jail, that some years subsequently it was turned over to the relatives of Booth, and buried in Mount Green Cemetery, Baltimore."

Captain E. W. Hilliard of Metropolis, Illinois, stated that he was one of four men who carried the remains from that jail, sinking it ten miles down the Potomac. Other witnesses are positive that the body was taken to a sandbar in the Potomac and "consumed in quick-lime." (70)

Ultimately, it was discovered that the corpse was buried in the dirt floor of the exercise portion of the penitentiary cell blocks of the Washington Arsenal. (71) When the arsenal was torn down, the body was moved and because of strong suspicion, re-identified by Colonel Pedgram and relatives (although Edwin Booth stayed in the corridor and refused to look).

Colonel Pedgram wrote: "The skin was drawn over the grinning skull, which showed the splendid teeth for which Booth was noted, there being only a single filling, which was identified by the dentist who did the work." (72) All three observers testified to the one filling.

However, a week before the murder, Dr. Merrill of Washington had filled a second tooth. (73) They could not have known this.

LIES AND COVER-UPS

John Parker watched the play for a while. As most other light comedies, *Our American Cousin* was corny. So he went for a stroll to the local bar. This would have been quite all right had he not been assigned to stand guard in front of a door behind which sat the President of the United States. One might wonder what happens to a man directly responsible for a President's assassination. In the case of John Parker—nothing. The Secretary of War kept him on. (74) In fact, it was found that Stanton withheld evidence at the Congressional investigation as to Parker's leaving his post. (75)

Yet Stanton was considered "chronically worried." He had arrested thirty-eight thousand people on flimsy evidence and suspended the right of habeus corpus. But there seems to have been one exception. At Mary Surratt's boarding house, John Wilkes Booth had been planning to kidnap Lincoln and exchange him for Confederate prisoners. (76)

Louis Weichman, a boarder there, became frightened and told a Captain Gleason who reported the plot to Provost Marshall Sharp. Weichman also told Captain McDavitt, the U.S. Enrolling Officer. By mid-March Stanton knew about the boarding house at 541 H. Street. Supposedly, detectives surveyed it for weeks. No daily report or habit of the boarders was ever reported. Neither

Gleason nor McDavitt were ever found again. (77)

Major Doherty wrote to headquarters asking why he, the commander of the regiment that went to Garrett's farm, was never asked to testify. His letter was "stored," but he received a five thousand dollar reward, the second biggest share of the money. (78)

The man in the barn had been shot with a pistol. But Boston Corbett had only a carbine. The pistol of the dead man, which was taken by the War Department, was never examined to find out whether one chamber was empty. (79) Stanton personally gave Corbett a pistol that the man carried to his many conferences on how he killed John Wilkes Booth. (80)

Immediately after finding the murderer's diary, Everton Conger (who received fifteen thousand dollars in reward, the largest share) galloped back to Washington and handed it to the Secretary of War. When it was finally discovered to be in Stanton's possession, the Congressional committee demanded that he surrender it to them, only to find that eighteen pages were missing.

The last line before the long gap reads: *Though I have greater desire, and almost a mind to return to Washington, and in a measure, clear my name—which I feel I can do.* (81) This little red diary withheld until 1867 led to the dismissal of Edwin M. Stanton. (82)

Lafayette C. Baker had one goal in mind: to assume as much credit as possible for trailing the fugitives and thereby receive most of the reward. The unanimous opinion of historians is summed up by Izola Forrester: "General Baker shrouded the burial of the man killed as Booth in the darkest mystery, and made the pursuit and shooting of the man in the Garrett barn a melodramatic travesty of vengeance to appease the shocked and clamorous North." (83)

On the floor of the Senate he was called "the greatest liar of them all" and it was added that "the baseness of his (Baker's) spurious coinage had no parallel in government annals." (84) He was dismissed under charges in July 1865 and returned home where he died before being brought to trial. (85) Nevertheless, as head of the Secret Service, by placing his seal of approval on the colorful, sensational stories of George Townsend, he gave them a certain official authority which has persisted down through the years.

5
THE SILENCE IS BROKEN

As the years went by, and important men passed away, oaths of sworn loyalty began to fade. The secrecy of the moment began to crack under the strain of time.

On March 31, 1922, because of a surge of opinion on the fate of the infamous actor, Joseph Ziegen and Wilson D. Kenzie, two of the soldiers at the Garrett farmhouse, swore in affidavits that when they saw the body carried from the barn, they stated that it was not Booth. They had seen him perform in New Orleans. Their testified that they were ordered to keep their mouths shut by the officers in command. (86)

In Forestville, California, Izola Forrester met with Elisha Shelburn Shortridge, the eighty-four year old grandson of Richard Garrett. Asked who the man was who was shot in the barn, he replied: "Always heard my folks say it was a Confederate soldier sent to warn the two men the troops were coming after them. Mosby's command wasn't far off, and it was some of his officers that brought Booth and the young feller to my grandfather....

"There must have been three (in the barn) because one gave himself up and one got shot and one got away. But it isn't good to talk about it to outsiders. My mother always said he must have had plenty of help." (87)

Asked about the testimony given by the Garrett family at the Conspiracy Trial, the old man chuckled: "Everyone was looking after his own skin, wasn't he? I can tell you this much. In those days and in my time up here, there was something bigger and mightier in this land than the law or government; something that bound men together in a tie of secret brotherhood stronger than family or country, even to the death. It stretched everywhere. You couldn't get away from it even if you wanted to...You never knew who belonged to it and who didn't, but it held the Southerners together." (88)

On June 22, 1900, Major Benton, commanding officer at the Washington Arsenal, lectured to the Army and Navy Club at New London, Connecticut. "We were requested by Secretary Stanton to remain silent, and no man during these thirty-five years has yet told." (89)

General O'Beirne, in his later years a judge presiding in City Hall Park in New York City, also talked with Mrs. Forrester in October of 1908:

"I can tell you something that has never been published in this case, and never even mentioned, something you will never find on any record. There were three men in that barn and one of them escaped...Think of how that place was padlocked carefully, and the key mislaid up at the house. It never was brought out in the testimony that there was another exit from the barn, but there was. Opening on the lower level at the rear was a small door, which gave direct egress to the ravine and woods.

"This was apparently overlooked while attention centered on the locked door in front...I intend to write a book around my early experiences some day. Maybe it will never be published until after I am dead, but that won't matter. We were all pledged to secrecy in those days. It was not safe to tell anything. Everyone was after a share of the reward. I received two thousand dollars myself." (90) Judge O'Beirne never lived to write his memoirs.

A FRIEND'S HELP

William Andrews, instrumental in the building of the Metropolitan Museum in Central Park and the Museum of Natural History in Manhattan Square, later president of the Erie Railway, told his daughter a strange story which she later recounted to Izola Forrester in 1926. He had been imprisoned for two years along with Dr. Mudd and others for having been a boyhood friend of Booth.

"Whether their meeting had been prearranged, she did not know, but her father had told her that he had met Booth after the actor had ridden away from Ford's Theater. Halting in his wild flight through the dark streets of Washington, he had told his friend what had happened, of his fall from the President's box, and the injury to his leg. It was causing him great pain, and her father had taken the silk cravat he wore around his own throat, and had bound the broken bone above the ankle with it, while Booth remained seated in the saddle. It required a secure fastening, and Billy had taken his own scarf-pin, and secured the improvised bandage with it. Booth rode away on his long dash down through Maryland, and her father never saw him again." (91)

Four years later he received a letter from San Diego. The feminine handwriting read: "In deepest gratitude for the kindness and succor given to my darling in his hour of distress." (92) With the letter was the cameo scarf-pin.

LETTERS FROM FAR AWAY

In 1868, according to Mrs. Forrester, her grandmother (Booth's common law wife) went to San Francisco with John Stevenson, Booth's close friend and a fellow member of the Knights of the Golden Circle. After a year she came back saying that the man she had met there had left for Asia. (93)

On April 14, 1865, Booth made his farewells to his family and left with his black servant, Henry. (94) In 1871, an actor named Kelley met Henry on Broadway. He was given an address in Asia. From then on the servant worked for Edwin Booth. A Colonel John Young, writing in the *Atlanta Journal* in 1924, claimed that he had read letters to Booth's close friend actor James Wells signed *John Wilkes* from Bombay, Calcutta, Shanghai, and Ceylon. (95)

On November 13, 1932 the son of James Wells, L.S. Wells, wrote to Izola Forrester and told her — I heard my father say many times, when I was a boy, "I know that John Wilkes Booth was never captured."

We must remember that Judah P. Benjamin, Secretary of War for the Confederacy, had been received in England with open arms and made Queen's Counsel. (96) Bombay had been taken over by the East India Company, and the new civil service list presented a solution to the placement of persons, especially Southern refugees. In 1865, Calcutta and Shanghai were strongholds of Freemasonry. (97)

The letters signed by Booth ceased to arrive in 1879. It is thought that the exiled man might have died that year, although there are intriguing stories of a man, known for his skill in reciting Shakespeare, who poisoned himself in Enid, Oklahoma in 1903, having stated that he was John Wilkes Booth.

A SON IS BORN

On March 23, 1870, Izola Mills d'Arcy and John Stevenson were married. Their son, Harry Jerome Dreshback Stevenson, had two different birthdates. Officially, it was February 27, 1871; in his mother's diary, it is listed as February 27, 1870. On his marriage certificate in Baltimore, he wrote down February 27, 1870. (98)

In 1918, the man who had given his name and security to the pregnant Izola whom he had accompanied to California, told his son as he lay dying: "But before we part, I think it is my duty to tell you something about yourself. You are not my son, Harry. You are the son of my friend, John Wilkes Booth." (99)

The pictures of Harry Stevenson look strikingly similar to those of Booth. "People remarked upon it, even strangers, and it annoyed him. He would always become aloof and very dignified when this resemblance was alluded to, and he did not like even the family to comment upon it." (100)

Constantly questioned and bothered by his curiosity-famined niece Izola Forrester (this writer's great-aunt), he once turned to her and said:

"Let the dead past bury its dead, my dear. You will do no good by dragging out family skeletons, or in trying to find out a secret which those we love have thought best to conceal. The lives of our mothers were shadowed by tragedy. Try and escape it as I do, by forgetting it. We have a new generation to consider in our children." (101)

CONCLUSION

There had been an attempt made on Secretary Stanton's life on April 14th, 1865. The would-be murderer rang the door bell and waited for his victim to answer. He never did. According to Stanton, his bell had been out of order for two or three days and the bellhanger had been too busy, although promptly notified. (102) Yet a reporter named Sterling said that when he came to give the Secretary of War the horrible news, the man's doorbell was working. (103)

It is also known that the afternoon of the 14th, John Wilkes Booth paid a visit to Vice President Andrew Johnson and, finding him absent, left him a card saying: "Don't want to disturb you. Are you at home." (104)

In 1867 it was discovered that Johnson, then governor, had met Booth in Nashville. (105) It was openly discussed in Congress that Johnson had "stood to benefit" by Lincoln's death. (106) Stanton had once met Booth through Johnson, and his private secretary admitted such an acquaintance. (108)

It may have been that the plots on Stanton and Johnson were decoys, to detract from the obvious suspicion that would fall on the Radical Republicans if the only men attacked were Lincoln and Seward, both of whom stood for Reconstruction. It may have been that the fugitive actor was helped by the Knights of the

Golden Circle whose octopus-like arms could have easily crossed the wires in the main battery in Washington D.C.

This research suggests that John Wilkes Booth was not a lone assassin; that similarly to the 1963 murder, there were immense forces that hovered over a deeply-hated, deeply-loved president. It is clear that Secretary Stanton's incriminating actions were geared toward catching anyone who could satisfactorily be passed off as the murderer in order to appease the turmoil in the country.

We may never prove conclusively that John Wilkes Booth fled the Garrett farmhouse and disappeared through the many routes opened by sympathizers, including those leading to foreign countries. But the evidence points to the fact that the official story is, to say the least, very suspicious. Family secrets have carried down through the years another story. Paradoxically, it witnesses to another sort of justice being carried out for the murder of one of this country's greatest presidents. Yet it also points toward strong probabilities of conspiracy that cannot be overlooked if we are to honor history through an honest search for truth.

Finally, the story of John Wilkes Booth remains a terrible personal tragedy regardless of his motives. A young man with a brilliant future ruined it all in the name of his political passions. Such a tale is not unfamiliar in our day when terrorist acts are rampant from Dublin to Oklahoma City. Perhaps the sad destiny of this once admired and adulated actor will stand as a reminder that violent acts can never be justified no matter the motive and that the price for such mistakes is all-consuming and unavoidable. May this family's dark secret keep others from choosing the wrong course of action.

NOTES

1. Philip Van Doren Stern, *The Man Who Killed Lincoln*, p. 357
2. Norman Kiell, *Psychological Studies of Famous Americans; The Civil War Era*, p. 138
3. James Truslow Adams, *The March of Democracy*, Vol. 3, p.172
4. Jim Bishop, *The Day Lincoln Was Shot*, p. 69
5. Izola Forrester, *This One Mad Act*, pp. 227-232
6. Stern, op.cit., p. 386
7. Forrester, op.cit., p. 118
8. Ibid., p. 357
9. Ibid., p. 369
10. Ibid., p. 369
11. Ibid., p. 371
12. Ibid.
13. Ibid., p. 360
14. Emma Lou Thornbrough, *Indiana In The Civil War Era 1850-1880*, p. 218
15. Ibid., p. 219
16. Forrester, op.cit., p. 368
17. Ibid., p. 344
18. Ibid.
19. Otto Eisenchiml, *Why Was Lincoln Murdered?*, p. 127
20. Ibid., p. 127

21. Ibid., p. 30

22. Ibid., p. 37

23. Ibid., p. 55

24. Ibid., p. 61

25. Ibid., p. 56

26. Ibid., p. 39

27. Ibid., p. 30

28. Bishop, op.cit., p. 252

29. Theodore Roscoe, *The Web of Conspiracy*, p. 183

30. Bishop, op.cit., p. 245

31. Eisenchiml, op. cit., p. 107

32. Forrester, op. cit. ,p. 292

33. Ibid., p. 286

34. Ibid., p. 283

35. Ibid., p. 286

36. Ibid., p. 289

37. Ibid., p. 288

38. Roscoe, op. cit., p. 394

39. Forrester, op. cit., p. 289

40. Ibid., p. 301

41. Eisenchiml, op. cit., p. 186

42. Forrester, op. cit., p. 293

43. Stern, op. cit., p. 403

44. Forrester, op. cit., p. 280

45. Ibid., p. 296

46. Ibid., p. 315

47. Ibid., p. 288

48. Ibid., p. 287

49. Otto Eisenchiml, *In the Shadow of Lincoln's Death*, p. 71

50. Ibid., p. 72

51. Forrester, op. cit., p. 435

52. Ibid., p. 436

53. Roscoe, op. cit., p. 396

54. Forrester, op. cit., p. 307

55. Stern, op. cit., p. 403

56. Roscoe, op. cit., p. 390

57. Bishop, op. cit., p. 300

58. Roscoe, op. cit., p. 425

59. Ibid., p. 427

60. Forrester, op. cit., p. 317

61. Roscoe, op. cit., p. 419

61a. Ibid., p. 425

62. Ibid., p. 426

63. Eisenchiml, *In the Shadow*, op. cit., p. 44

64. Roscoe, op. cit., p. 420

65. Forrester, op. cit., p. 313

66. Eisenchiml, *In the Shadow*, op. cit., p. 43

67. Bryan, *The Great American Myth*, p. 275

68. Forrester, op. cit., p. 246

69. Roscoe, op. cit., p. 423

70. Forrester, op. cit., p. 307

71. *Album of the Lincoln Murder*, p. 48

72. Roscoe, op. cit., p. 529

73. Ibid., p. 529

74. Ibid.

75. Eisenchiml, *W hy Was Lincoln Murdered?*, p. 30

76. Forrester, op. cit., p. 234

77. Bishop, op. cit., p. 82

78. Roscoe, op. cit., p. 140

79. Eisenchiml, *Why Was Lincoln Murdered?*, p. 157

80. *Album of the Lincoln Murder,* op. cit., p. 51
81. Forrester, op. cit., p. 356
82. Ibid., p. 441
83. Ibid., p. 292
84. Ibid., p. 293
85. Ibid., p. 294
86. Ibid., p. 299
87. Ibid., p. 464
88. Ibid., p. 465
89. Ibid., p. 317
90. Ibid., p. 304
91. Ibid., p. 425
92. Ibid., p. 115
93. Ibid., p. 115
94. Ibid., p. 382
95. Ibid.
96. Ibid., p. 396
97. Ibid., p. 437
98. Ibid., p. 111
99. Ibid., p. 108
100. Ibid., p. 109
101. Ibid., p. 108
102. Eisenchiml, *In the Shadow,* op. cit., p. 358
103. Ibid., p. 359
104. Roscoe, op. cit., p. 182
105. Ibid., p. 182
106. Stern, op. cit., p. 399
107. Eisenchiml, *Why Was Lincoln Murdered?,* p. 436

BIBLIOGRAPHY

Adams, James Truslow, *The March of Democracy, Vol. 3, Civil War and Reconstruction*, New York: Charles Scribner's Sons, 1932.

Bishop, Jim, *The Day Lincoln Was Shot*, New York: Harper and Brothers, 1955.

Borreson, Ralph, *When Lincoln Died*, New York: Appleton-Century, 1965.

Bryan, George, *The Great American Myth*, New York: Garrick and Evans, Inc. 1940.

Eisenchiml, Otto, *Why Was Lincoln Murdered?*, Boston: Little, Brown and Company, 1937.

Eisenchiml, Otto, *In the Shadow of Lincoln's Death*, New York: Wilfred Fink Inc., 1940.

Forrester, Izola, *This One Mad Act*, Boston: Hale, Cushman and Flint, 1937.

Kiell, Norman, *Psychological Studies of Famous Americans: The Civil War Era*, New York: Twayne Publishing, Inc., 1964.

Roscoe, Theodore, *The Web of Conspiracy*, Englewood Cliffs, New Jersey: Prentice-Hall,Inc., 1959.

Sandburg, Carl, *Abraham Lincoln - The War Years IV, Vol. 6*, New York: Charles Scribner's Sons, 1939,

Stern, Philip Van Doren, *The Man Who Killed Lincoln*, New York: The Literary Guild of America, Inc., 1939.

Thornbrough, Emma Lou, *Indiana In the Civil War Era 1850-1880*, Indianapolis, Indiana Historical Bureau & Indiana Historical Society, 1965.

Album of the Lincoln Murder: Illustrating how it was planned, committed and avenged. (Historical Times, Inc.) Harrisburg, Pennsylvania: Stackpole Books, 1965

ABOUT THE AUTHOR

Theodore J. Nottingham is an author of fiction and non-fiction books that cover the spectrum from historical novels to works on spirituality. His articles are regularly featured in a variety of national and regional magazines. He is also a television and video producer and has authored a number of screenplays. Mr. Nottingham lives in the Midwest with his wife and daughter.